Cow Palace · 3 MINUTES FROM CANDLESTICK PARK
Open 24 Hours
LANES
NUE · SAN FRANCISCO · JUNIPER 6-9550
Close Cover Before Striking

20 AUTOMATIC LANES OPEN ALL NIGHT
Cherry BOWL

Civic LANES
234 PICO BLVD. SANTA MONICA, CALIF.
EXbrook 9-7731
Also the exclusive
Civic Club

288
"Top of the Quad" CLAIREMONT, CALIFORNIA
BELLFLOWER

DIckens 5-5250
TARZANA, CALIFORNIA
Corbin BOWL
OPEN 24 HOURS

DA. 3-7373
Del Mar
LANES
12900 S. CRENSHAW GARDENA, CALIF.
Close Cover Before Striking

HAVE A STRIKE ON COBRA BOWL

Country Club Lanes
2600 WATT AVE. SACRAMENTO · CALIFORNIA

Phone TO 1-0991
Del Rio LANES
7502 E. FLORENCE DOWNEY, CALIF.
Close Cover Before Striking

bowl
ERNARDINO RD. ALIFORNIA

Phone TE 5-8237
COVE BOWL
Close Cover Before Striking

BOWLING
Divine Gardens STEAK HOUSE
TURLOCK, CALIFORNIA
Close Cover Before Striking

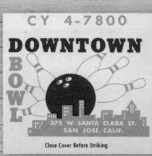

CY 4-7800
DOWNTOWN BOWL
375 W. SANTA CLARA ST. SAN JOSE, CALIF.
Close Cover Before Striking

JE 7-0950
FUTURAMA LANES
9757 GARDEN GROVE BLVD. GARDEN GROVE, CALIF.
Close Cover Before Striking

Phone TO 6-9757
BOWL
DUTCH VILLAGE
Bowling Center
Close Cover Before Striking

Gregory Lanes
16 beautiful automatic lanes
JOIN A LEAGUE
"Where Bowlers Send Their Friends"
LION MATCH CO. INC. LOS ANGELES, CAL.

Mardi Gras Lanes
MADISON & OAK AVE. SACRAMENTO, CALIF.
Close Cover Before Striking

BOWL 32 BEAUTIFUL LANES
Friendly Hills Bowl
15545 WHITTIER BLVD. EAST WHITTIER, CALIF.

Futurama
42 LANES
CHerry 8-8150
BOWL

IT'S THE VOGUE TO BOWL
COCKTAILS CAFE
LOS ANGELES

Indio Bowl
BOWLING PANCAKE HOUSE COCKTAILS DINING
44503 JACKSON STREET
Indio CALIFORNIA

HOLLYWOOD 9-3111
HOLLYWOOD LEGION Lanes
In the Heart of Hollywood

Bowl 36 LANES
HOLIDAY BOWL
3730 CRENSHAW BLVD. LOS ANGELES, CALIF.
CLOSE COVER BEFORE STRIKING

8 ACRES · FREE PARKING
Picwood BOWL
GRANITE 8-0751
WEST LOS ANGELES
CLOSE COVER BEFORE STRIKING

NORMANDIE 5-4111
Hollywood Star Lanes

521-1241
La Mirada
BOWL
36 LANES
CLOSE COVER BEFORE STRIKIN

	NAME	HANDICAP	1	2	3	4	5	6	7	8	9	10	TOTAL
1													
2													
3													
4													
5													
6		TOTAL											
7		HANDICAP											
8													
9													
10													
11													
12		TOTAL											

BOWLING TERMS
STRIKE ☒ FOUL
SPARE ☑ CHERRY
BLOW ⊟ TURKEY ⊠
SPLIT ◯ DOUBLE ⊠
SPLIT MADE ⊠

FIVE GOOD IDEAS

1 RESPECT THE EQUIPMENT

2 DON'T LOFT BALL

3 OBSERVE FOUL LINES

4 OBSERVE BOWLING ETIQUETTE

Bowl Your Own
Brunswick
MINERALITE
the Bowling Ball with
DYNAMIC BALANCE
FOR MORE PINS...MORE FUN

ALLEY NO.
SHEET 40118

BOWLERO
Ladies' Day Leagues
Nursery for Children
Always Open Play

BOWLARAMA

THE ARCHITECTURE OF MID-CENTURY BOWLING

BOWLARAMA

THE ARCHITECTURE OF MID-CENTURY BOWLING

CHRIS NICHOLS WITH ADRIENE BIONDO

ANGEL CITY PRESS · LOS ANGELES PUBLIC LIBRARY

BOWL WHERE YOU SEE THE
"MAGIC **AMF** TRIANGLE"

AMF

467-E   FUN FOR ALL   © A. SCHEER   LITHO IN U.S.A.

A "Fun For All" promotion from AMF brings the nuclear family to the atomic age bowling center.

300 Bowl (1958, Powers, Daly & DeRosa) in Phoenix is the work of master bowling architects at the peak of their creativity.

A rendering of Kapu Kai (1962, Talley-Guevara Associates), a Polynesian modernist fantasy rising up out of the vineyards of Cucamonga, some forty miles east of Los Angeles. ◆ Inset: Color postcard of the Kapu Kai shows the reality of what was built: a dramatic combination of breeze block and extreme gables in a tropical-meets-desert landscaping.

KAPU-KAI

DINING — DANCING — BOWLING

8874 Foothill Blvd., Cucamonga, Calif. — Hwy. 66

TALLEY-GUEVARA
ASSOCIATES
ARCHITECTS

A rendering shows off the ultramodern design planned for Del Amo Lanes (1959, Anthony and Langford) in Torrance, California.
The forty-lane center included a coffee shop, dining room and banquet facility, and a children's play area.
Of special note was the revolving bar in the cocktail lounge.

An island oasis along Pacific Coast Highway in Long Beach, California, Java Lanes (1958, Powers, Daly & DeRosa) utilized organic materials like stone and exposed woodwork, inside and out.

A massive porte cochere, like the one marking the entrance of Friendly Hills Bowl (1957, Powers, Daly & DeRosa), in Whittier, California, became a signature element of the firm's designs. ◆ Opposite: A side view of Bel Mateo Bowl (1957, Powers, Daly & DeRosa) in San Mateo, California, shows off the exuberant colors and lighting effects that attracted crowds twenty-four hours a day.

...GO BOWLING!

"It's Cool...It's Fun...Go Bowling!" AMF invited friends and families everywhere to get out there and bowl.

INTRODUCTION

Color rendering of the [...] Mission Hills, California, designed by architect Martin Stern Jr. in 1957, [...] incorporated Googie [...] "Swiss cheese" I-beams.

BOWLING IS THE MOST POPULAR participation sport in the United States. Yes, deep into our twenty-first century, handheld, streaming, AI world, more Americans roll a heavy ball at ten pins than engage in football, baseball, or soccer. The United States Bowling Congress reports that sixty-seven million of us take to the lanes each year, and it's been that way for generations. Bowling is a $10 billion industry because most people actually play the game rather than watch others do it.

Bowling attracts men and women, young and old, rich and poor. It's the great equalizer and has the widest possible range of players. A century ago it was still a saloon sport, mostly

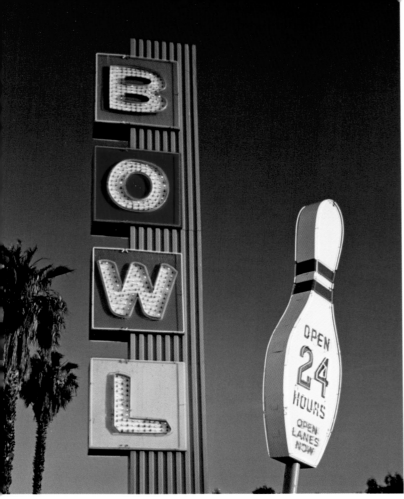

Linbrook Bowl (1958, Schwager, Desatoff & Henderson), not far from Disneyland, was built by Stuart A. "Stu" Bartleson and Larkin Donald "L.D." Minor of the Atlantic and Pacific Building Corporation. A large-scale neon extravaganza, Linbrook's oversized bowling pin sign still revolves into the wee hours.

played by rowdy men in urban settings. After World War II, a concerted effort was made to reform the game and attract more players, and it worked.

Technological and social changes completely reinvented the experience, and bowling exploded in popularity during the 1950s and '60s. Several factors, from the invention of the automatic pinsetter to the development of the suburbs to the changing family dynamics of the postwar years, led to an arms race among bowling proprietors to outspend each other and capture a bigger audience, each of them splurging deliriously on ever larger and more lavish pin palaces at the edge of town. Hundreds of architectural confections rose up with amenities slathered on like buttercream frosting. These fanciful fun zones appeared like mini resorts along the highways stringing together the new towns, jazzing up the 'burbs with their fanciful names, make-believe buildings, lush landscaping, and colossal neon signs. The trend started in California, and this casual glamour and popular luxury spread nationwide.

When the American Bowling Congress chose Los Angeles as the site for its 1947 tournament, boosters noted that the number of local bowling establishments had grown in a decade from twelve to 166, and that at "no place in the United States has the game enjoyed greater growth and increase in popularity than in Southern California." At bowling's peak in the 1960s, there were more than 10,000 centers nationwide, and almost 10% of them were in California. That same year, President Harry S. Truman installed the first bowling lanes under the White House, and soon after, lavish new space age bowling centers began to bloom all over America.

During the boom years, some 25% of the

population considered themselves bowlers, and athletes who played the sport professionally earned more than NFL players. The bowling lane is where Americans of vastly different backgrounds can come together to play with one another. The last time I bowled, a lawyer and an ex-con faced off against each other. The group also included a magician and at least three actors, but it *was* Hollywood.

The lavish new space age bowling centers that began to bloom all over America were sumptuous sports palaces designed to catch your eye, draw you in, and keep you entertained all day and night. The architecture joined with the restaurants, motels, and drive-in theaters on the burgeoning roadside strip—all competing with each other to produce the most arresting rooflines and brightest neon signs, soaring into the night and reflecting their liquid fire off the chrome, glass, and tail fins of the showiest cars to ever roll out of Detroit. The oversized signs were beacons of light and excitement on roads cutting through what had previously been agricultural land, miles from the big city.

The arresting forms and space age shapes employed to catch the eye are known as googie architecture. The style was named for Googies coffee shop in Hollywood, designed by architect John Lautner in 1947. Lautner trained with Frank Lloyd Wright and moved to Los Angeles where he became a legendary modern architect, crafting organic mas-

Left to right: Helen Quijano, her daughter Cristy, and Cristina Gonzalez at the Plaza Bowl (1959, Powers, Daly & DeRosa) before it opened in National City, California, 1958.

terpieces from concrete and steel, not to mention the homes of the rich-and-famous hidden in the hills and seen mostly in architecture magazines. He didn't talk much about his early work, which stood out among California's already dynamic and stylish roadside wonders. Architects Louis Armet and Eldon Davis built on Lautner's ideas to craft increasingly sophisticated coffee shops with

Top: Structural A-frames punctuate a modern floating roof in this 1961 Armet & Davis architectural rendering for the Starlite Bowl in Reno, Nevada. ◆ Bottom: The low-slung lines of the 1958 Stardust Bowl in Watsonville, California, designed by Armet & Davis.

in the 1990s, hitting the lanes in *King Ralph* (1991), *The Flintstones* (1994), and *The Big Lebowski* (1998), as well as the TV league on *Roseanne*.

In the ensuing decades, most of the exciting mid-century buildings disappeared and the sport remade itself into a $5 billion industry, embracing trends like blacklight bowling, live DJs, and gourmet food delivered to the lanes. In 1994, Tom Shannon revived the grimy Bowlmor in Greenwich Village with these luxury amenities. His Bowlero Corporation has become a bowling behemoth with hundreds of locations that completely dominates a transformed industry.

Whether you remember a googie bowling alley from childhood birthday parties, as an architectural anomaly that captured your imagination, or if you are one of the lucky ones who was able to visit these places at the peak of their power, experiencing the architecture in real life is far different than reading about it as art. These explosive buildings were written off as kitsch, but their architecture has transcended the slur with expert craftsmanship, a perfectly suited purpose, and a sophisticated whimsy.

Googie captures the compressed energy and enthusiasm of a generation that finally got to build a great big beautiful tomorrow. "Of course those of my generation were ex-

cited beyond measure with the opportunities available to us with postwar America," remembered engineer Richard Bradshaw, who helped craft some of the icons of the era. "We had just lived through eleven years of Depression plus four years of war. We now thought we could do anything we set our minds to doing. It was a very heady feeling after the dreary years when we saw no end to the Depression and a possible terrible end to the war . . . So this was the time for California, and especially Los Angeles, to burst forth with exuberance, which it did."

We are thrilled to share this lost world with you. Welcome to *Bowlarama*.

The whole family admires mom's modern bowling trophy. May, 1968. ◆ Opposite: A group of kids enjoy a meal in a postwar bowling alley coffee shop in a scene captured for *Life* magazine in 1958.

CHAPTER 1

HISTORY

This nineteenth-century glass slide depicts medieval peasants enjoying an early version of bowling.

DOES BOWLING PREDATE THE human race? Ancient hominids crafted their first balls some two million years ago. Scientists debate the purpose of the artifacts found at archaeological sites in Africa, Europe, and Asia, suggesting they were used as weapons or as tools to grind up plants. Researchers examining specimens in Israel discovered they were used to crush bone to extract the marrow inside. Some believe they might have been artworks. There is a lot left to learn about these spheres, but what we do know is that they would have rolled. We might imagine ancients playing or practicing skills that would be useful in a hunt.

Left: Stone Age artifacts reveal a bowling-like game that involved rolling rounded stones at sheep's bones. ◆ Right: Ancient balls and pins were discovered in Egypt by Sir Flanders Petrie in 1939.

Games and sports are an essential part of every culture. Literature from the Middle Ages indicates that rounded stones were used as balls and bones were used as pins in a game called *Loggats*, an early precursor to bowling, a game still popular in Shakespeare's time. Perhaps Stone Age revelers threw or rolled their stone balls at broken bones as well.

Bowling has an ancient lineage that developed over millennia to slowly become the game it is today, from stones and bones to a game enjoyed by kings and queens, from rolling greens and seedy taverns to the metropolises of light and synchronized play that define the modern bowling alley.

The earliest archeological artifacts from a game that resembles bowling date back to ancient Egypt. In 1939, former professor of Egyptology at the University of London, Sir Flinders Petrie, revealed that he found a complete set of bowling paraphernalia in a child's tomb dating to 5200 BC. He found wall drawings of the sport as well as several small stone balls and nine slender pins. In the fifth century, Herodotus documented bowling and dice games played by the Ancient Greeks. Westerners visiting Hawaii in the eighteenth century saw islanders rolling disc-shaped stones in the game they called *ula maika*, as they had for hundreds of years. The invading Romans,

Left: Lithograph by Bartolomeo Pinelli and Charles Joseph Hullmandel showing young Romans playing Ruzzolo, a game similar to bowling with round discs. ◆ Right: King Henry VIII and his courtiers at Whitehall in 1530.

who conquered what is now Switzerland, played a game similar to modern bocce ball.

Modern bowling originated in European cathedrals, where parishioners would line up a row of club-like weapons called *kegels*, imagine they were "heathens," and roll a ball to knock them down. If they were successful, they were declared pious and celebrated at a special dinner. If not, they needed to attend church more regularly. As early as 1174, spectators in London gathered to watch athletes throw stones at pins, and soon bowlers in Germany, Holland, and Switzerland had started bowling on wood instead of grass. They threw their stones down a long narrow plank with a wider platform at the end to hold the pins. These types of alleys still exist in Germany. In 1301, the first game of "bowls," which shared a common lineage with bowling, curling, and shuffleboard, was played on the oldest surviving bowling green in England adjoining the God's House Hospital.

Byzantine rules over the number of pins, as well as the size of balls and where to roll them, varied from region to region, but nevertheless, the game became more popular than ever. In 1361, King Edward III outlawed the game entirely as he felt his archers were spending too much time bowling and too little time getting ready for war. Richard II expanded the law to include the game called *gettre de peer* (throwing the stones) in 1388. By 1477, Edward IV passed another law banning ball rolling games including "closh," "kailes," and "queekboard" with a punishment of three years in prison. The law cited gambling as the cause of "murders, robberies, and other heinous felonies" happening near "places where they use and occupy their said ungracious and incommendable games."

No matter how regulators tried to stop the sport, people kept bowling, although some aristocrats scorned the game. Sir Thomas Elyot wrote that skittles and ring toss were "utterly objected of all noble men." In 1541, Henry VIII changed the law so that only the wealthy could bowl. The Unlawful Games Act said that "Bowyers" should not suffer from "many subtil inventative and crafty Persons" who kept a place of bowling for "Gaine, Lucre, or Living." Meaning that no one who had to charge for bowling would be allowed to provide it. The law went on to say that "no Manner of Artificer or Craftsman of any Handicraft or Occupation, Husbandman, Apprentice, Labourer, Servant at Husbandry, Journeyman, or Servant Artificer, Mariners, Fisherman, Watermen, any Serving-Man

In a tavern, men drink at the table or play *quilles*, a game similar to bowling. Painting by Victor Marec from *L'Illustration*, 1892.

Martin Olson's bowling alley in Kent, Washington, 1903.

shall at any Time play at any Bowl or Bowls in open Places out of Christmas." The law did, however, allow for games (including tennis and bowling) to be played at manors with a value of "1000 pounds or above." The law had the side effect of opening up great houses to the sport. Henry VIII certainly took advantage of his own law, adding "fair-tennice-courtes, bowling-alleys, and a cock-pit" to Whitehall, his royal palace.

As London urbanized throughout the eighteenth century, it became more difficult to find open greens for archery or outdoor bowls. British historian Joseph Strutt noted that people's only resource for physical exercise was "skittles, Dutch pins, four corners and the like pastimes" that were mostly available in taverns and drinking houses. Because of the rough nature of these places, he recounts a judge in the 1700s removing all the skittles frames and prohibiting the games.

Although there were constant threats to the game, there were also improvements. Some say that lawn bowling was saved by the Scots, who created a uniform set of regulations and designed carefully laid out and maintained lawns in private clubs. In Germany, the game called *kegeling*, enjoyed by Martin Luther, was considered wholesome. The famed theologian built an alley for his children, and they bowled together as a family. Luther's enthusiasm also helped to standardize practices in Germany, when, after experimenting, he decided ninepins made the best game.

Wooden balls replaced stone, and were made from lignum vitae, imported to Europe from the Caribbean in the early 1500s. All balls were originally shaped by hand, and no two were alike. Thomas Taylor, founder of Taylor Bowls, patented a machine that would shape balls consistently, making a set of four out of a single log of lignum vitae. The Scottish family-owned company was founded in 1796 and still operates today. Lignum vitae was replaced by composition balls in the twentieth century, partly due to the rarity of the wood. Wooden balls were carefully made slightly flat on one side in order to move along a curved path. This curve is called a bias. Although this bias might have originally been accidental when stones were used, it became a matter of pride because controlling the bias required much greater skill to master the game. The bias is still created in modern bowling balls today. Harry Alten, who was a pinboy in Chicago in 1891, remembered what it was like bowling with a wooden ball:

> Lignum vitae bowling balls really were something . . . They lasted only about six months or a year, if you were lucky. They were hard on the hands. The wood slivered, especially around the finger and thumb holes.

BOWLING GREEN, NEW YORK CITY

Bowling Green, located at the foot of Broadway, is New York City's oldest park, designated in 1733. Tavern owners would provide balls and pins to their customers for use at public bowling greens.

You could tell a bowler by all the splinters in his hands.

North American bowling history started at the British settlement of Jamestown in 1611. The aristocratic British loved their bowling greens and this nomenclature shows up to this day in the names of cities and towns in Ohio, Kentucky, Virginia, and Missouri, as well as the oldest park in Lower Manhattan.

The little park that lies at the foot of Broadway and is still called Bowling Green was founded in 1733 by John Chambers, Peter Baynard, and Peter Jay, who leased the former parade grounds near a fort.

Bowling was very popular in nineteenth-century American pop culture, and shows up in political cartoons and the storyline of classic books like Washington Irving's *Rip Van*

Gentlemen engaged in a game of bowling, circa 1894.

Winkle. The title character is awakened from his decades-long sleep by a game of ninepins. However, the proliferation of gambling at bowling greens caused several states to outlaw ninepin bowling. Connecticut, from its early days as a British colony, had laws against "Dice, Cards, Tables, Bowles, Shuffleboard, Billiards, Coytes, Keiles, Loggets, or any other implements, used in gaming" and was one of the first states to classify ninepins as gambling in 1841, quickly followed by Massachusetts and New York.

These bans are thought to have created the American-style tenpin bowling, which added a pin and changed their arrangement from a diamond into a triangle layout. The inventors of the new game probably didn't notice the line in Connecticut law noting that "nine pin alleys prohibited whether more or less pins are used on penalty of a fine not exceeding $50.00." Tenpin bowling accounts for 95% of the bowling done in the United States today. (Duckpin and candlepin bowling are variants with smaller pins and balls, and are still popular in some regions.)

The game also moved indoors, probably due, in part, to the bans, but also partially due to an influx of German immigrants who brought their style of bowling to New York. The city's Germantown bloomed in the 1820s, and a decade later bowling clubs appeared in many eastern cities. The Knickerbocker was the first indoor alley; it opened in 1840. Soon, indoor alleys seemed to pop up on nearly every block of Broadway from Fulton to 14th Street, and on various parts of the Bowery. The Roseland Cottage bowling alley in Woodstock, Connecticut, was built in 1846 and survives today. Even though you can't bowl there, the National Historic Landmark is open for tours.

John Cleveland, aka "Tenpin Johnny," and Richard Pheany were two of the first stars of the sport and both opened saloons in New York. Bowling began to come into vogue with the upper classes, as wealthy industrialists and other elites incorporated small alleys into their own mansions and bowled at private clubs and upscale resorts. And, not for the last time, an appeal to women was made as an 1855 Milwaukee newspaper indicates:

> The lady who passed through Burns's swinging doors, took a short look at the joint and told the proprietor it would never do if you wanted the feminine trade. Spittoons went out, the genuine oil paintings of naked nymphs came down from behind the bar, curtains were hung, and rugs laid. Signs went up asking gents to kindly refrain from profane language and shave twice a week.

Top: A nineteenth-century illustration depicting King Edward VII bowling at Sandringham House. ◆ Center: Color postcard illustrated by Carl Thiel. ◆ Bottom: A group portrait shows nine members of the Chicago Bowling Team at a bowling alley in Chicago, circa 1901.

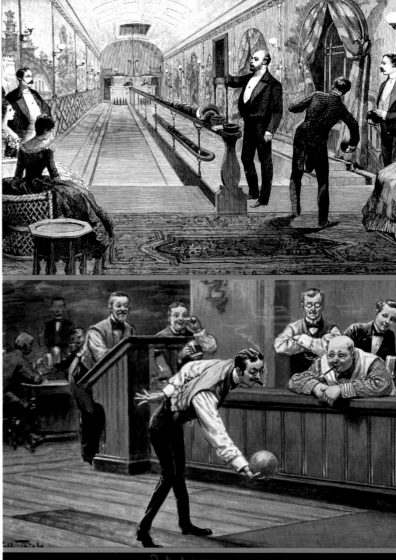

Top: Bowlers on the southside of Chicago, documented in 1941. Bottom: A bowler proud of his perfect 300 game admires his score on a chalk scoreboard in McClean County, Illinois, during the 1930s.

Just because the game had ten pins laid out in a triangle doesn't mean it was like our game today. The pins were gigantic and set close together. It was so easy to bowl a 300 that fans soured on the pastime and billiards became more popular.

Brunswick Bros., a billiard table manufacturing company, was founded in Cincinnati in 1845 by John M. Brunswick and his half brothers, David and Emanuel. In the mid-1850s, they expanded to Chicago, St. Louis, New Orleans, and other cities. Brunswick started manufacturing bowling equipment in the 1880s and continues to this day.

A failed revolution in Germany in 1848 started the next big wave of immigration, and almost one million Germans soon came to America. This idealistic wave of Germans were strong believers in physical as well as cultural education, establishing gymnasiums in their new communities called *Turnverein*, which housed all the entertainments popular in Germany, including bowling. The German enthusiasm for health might have been one of the reasons that, prior to the Civil War, Americans shed their puritanical ideals that frowned on play.

The sports-conscious America we know today got its start in the second half of the nineteenth century. Cities began dedicating more land for public use, including beaches and parks. By the 1880s, churches began to see recreation as a way to fend off vice, and started providing gymnasiums and

Left: The deplorable conditions young pinboys had to work under were documented by the National Child Labor Committee. Frank Jarose, Joseph Philip, and Willie Payton, all eleven years old, worked every day until midnight at Les Miserables bowling alley in Lowell, Massachusetts. Philip reported earning as little as $1.75 a week. ◆ Right: Photo taken at 11:30 pm shows the small boys employed at this center in Syracuse, New York.

promoting games and concerts rather than forbidding them on the Sabbath after church. And at the turn of the century, sports became part of the high school curriculum.

In the 1860s, through the persistent efforts of German Americans on the East Coast, bowling flourished and began to move West. The Baltimore *schützengesellschaft* (shooting club) featured dance floors, bowling alleys, banquet rooms, and a park that hosted up to twenty thousand people. A turn-of-the-century bowler remembered how bowling in Chicago looked in this period: "The only boys were Germans, and the only alleys were the very crude ones at the picnic groves and other German resorts. When we wanted to bowl, we made up a party of our friends, ladies, and gentlemen, hired a wagon, and drove ten, fifteen or twenty miles to one of our favorite picnic gardens."

The earliest record of bowling in California was in 1866 in the redwood forests of Sonoma County, when a group of men cut down an enormous tree, shaved the topside flat, created a shed over one end of the log, and bowled wooden balls or stones down the tree toward wooden blocks at the other end.

Bowling clubs formed in New York, and tournaments pitting clubs against each other followed. There were many variants of tenpins played, and some alleys measured one hundred feet in length. The diameter of the balls also varied, ranging from four to nine inches, and they didn't have finger holes. In the original German games, the pins were not set up after each ball. That changed with the formation of the National Bowling Association (NBA) in 1875.

in the country a decade later. Vince Hayes, who built Bimini Bowl, also opened Rialto Recreation in San Francisco in 1928, the first bowling alley with wall-to-wall plush carpeting. Suddenly, large numbers of women and white-collar workers felt comfortable going out to bowl. In 1914, there were seventy-five thousand bowlers in Chicago, but even with prohibition, by the mid-1920s the number had more than quadrupled.

Bowling was not immune from the effects of the Great Depression. In January 1936, Brunswick reported that it had repossessed more bowling lanes than it had sold in the New York area. Private investors continued to build new centers. "When I came to San Antonio from Minnesota in 1926, the German influence was strong and most of the bowling there was ninepins. I got them into tenpins," recalled Mrs. Violet "Billy" Simon. "Owners made most of their money off bars, so they didn't pay much attention to their lanes. The things that got women to bowl were that the places were cleaned up, classes were held so

A Brunswick showplace, the Hollywood Recreation Center at Sunset and Vine (1937, Walker & Eisen), was designed in the Streamline Moderne style popular in the late 1930s.

they can [sic] learn the game, and they were made welcome. Knowing they were welcome was very important to women."

In 1931, Ora Forman opened the San Jose Bowling Palace which, the *San Jose Mercury Herald* announced, was "a new temple of sport: twelve slick alleys, the newest modern equipment perfectly lighted; one of the finest on the Pacific Coast," whose amenities included dressing rooms, showers, a barber shop, soda fountain, and cigar stand.

After Prohibition was repealed at the end of 1933, bowling continued to modernize and professionalize. There was a resurgence in bowling in the Midwest when breweries such as Pabst and Schlitz sponsored promotional "beer teams" that toured the country. *Bowling* magazine, published by the ABC, launched in 1934, joining *Bowlers Journal* started by Dave Luby in 1913, which remains the oldest sporting journal in America. Air conditioning brought in new customers and would become integral to modern bowling centers. Hayes Rialto Recreation in Fresno,

Byron Thomas's evocative painting *Pastime Bowling Alley*, 1939.

California, was the first in the state to offer air conditioning.

The 1939 opening of the Sunset Bowling Center on Hollywood's Sunset Boulevard kicked off a banner year. Located in the former headquarters of Warner Bros. studios, on the stages where Al Jolson made the first talking picture, the bowling center was the largest in the world at the time, with fifty lanes. The sports palace offered more than just tenpins; it also had badminton courts, a skating rink, and a loft where the pinboys lived. That same year, construction started on the sleek, Streamline Moderne Hollywood Recreation Center. Eight movie studios put in applications for league bowling at the new hot spot at Sunset and Vine in 1939.

Rick Golobic remembers his grandparents' stories of owning a bowling alley in San Francisco before going down to Los Angeles to work at their new center:

Henry and Inez Golobic opened the first street-level bowling center in the Western United States. It was like a grocery at street level and the family lived upstairs. On the third floor were

rooms they rented out, and down below was a very holy place. During Prohibition, a lot of Catholics gathered there to partake of the Jesuits' altar wine. They prayed for the police officers who frequented the (Downtown Bowl) as well.

The family took their expertise to Southern California and reinvented the game: In 1937, my grandfather decided to sell his grocery store and bar, and whatever else. It was on Portrero Hill in San

Top: A man and woman with the Japanese American Citizens League pose for a photo with their bowling trophies; Seattle, 1958. ◆ Left: In 1941, silent-era film star Harold Lloyd joined with pro-bowling partners Ned Day and Hank Marino and built the Llo-Da-Mar Bowl (1941, Douglas Lee) in Santa Monica, California.

Francisco and somebody at Brunswick contacted him and asked if he was interested in going into business. They basically took all their assets and put them into Hollywood Recreation Center, which was influential. Lines around the block. It was Brunswick's showplace. It was street level. Not a smoke-filled basement. Not a walk down…street level was a big deal, number one. Now they were open to everybody, people could see in, and you didn't cover the windows. Now you had literally hundreds of pictures of Hollywood movie stars at Hollywood Recreation Center.

Harold Lloyd's studio team, along with other movie stars, frequented the Hollywood

Top: Baseball legend Yogi Berra and fellow New York Yankees star Phil Rizzuto were among the many sports stars to invest in a bowling center. Their Rizzuto-Berra Lanes (1958, Emil A. Schmidlin) opened in Clifton, New Jersey, with a bar shaped like Yankee Stadium. ◆ Bottom: Woodley Lewis at the controls of his new Sportsman's Bowl (1961, Powers, Daly & DeRosa) in Compton, California.

(NNBA) was formed in Detroit a decade later. Vel Scott, wife of bowler Don Scott who was named an "Unsung Hero" by the Congressional Black Caucus for helping to integrate bowling, reminisced about the mixed feelings of the African American community at the time. "J. Elmer Reed and Virgil Brown started the National Negro Bowling Association. Why try to integrate? Just do your own thing."

Five years later, this group was renamed The National Bowling Association (TNBA) because its membership included a diverse group of people of color such as Asians, Latinos, and Native Americans. During this

Recreation Center. They were also spotted at the Riverside Bowling Academy in Palm Springs, whose proprietor, Ludie Britsch, taught Harold Lloyd and Ralph Bellamy to bowl, and whose opening night included stars like Humphrey Bogart. Lloyd and pro-bowling partners Ned Day and Hank Marino opened their own center, Llo-Da-Mar Bowl in Santa Monica in 1941.

The ABC was still restricted to white men. Women had defiantly formed their own organization, the WNBA, in 1916, which also limited membership to white people. Bowlers of Japanese ancestry born in the United States (called Nisei) in Seattle, San Francisco, and Fresno came together to form the Japanese American Citizens League in 1929, and the National Negro Bowling Association

period, Black and white people were not only bowling separately, they were living separately as well. Two Supreme Court rulings, in 1948 and 1953, declared housing covenants unconstitutional, and it was not until the 1968 Fair Housing Act that they were finally enforceable. The NNBA fought for equity in bowling as many others were fighting for equity around the nation. At least the ABC and WIBC didn't wait until the 1960s to integrate; they both removed the restrictive clauses from their constitutions in 1950.

Bowling became even more popular during World War II, even though the ABC national tournament, held annually from 1901 to 1942, was canceled during wartime. Bowling became one of the recreational activities provided on military bases and champions toured the enlisted men's camps. This was a boon to Brunswick, which had suffered during the Depression. The company installed more than thirteen thousand billiards tables and three thousand bowling lanes at military bases during the war. Brunswick was chosen because it was also providing Congress with new alloys for aircraft as well as other high-tech products, including floating mines, fuselages, landing skids for gliders, bomb flares for night bombing raids, assault boats, and more.

The US considered taxing bowling, but the ABC convinced the government that it was bad for the national economy and wartime morale. Once the industry realized that

The United States Public Health Service issued a series of posters at the start of World War II reminding soldiers of the importance of sleep, safety, and recreation.

bowling could assist the war effort, it founded the Bowlers Victory Legion (BVL) in 1942 and began sending cards and games to servicemen, and later provided therapeutic programs and services, including adaptive equipment on the lanes to help disabled veterans play the game. The National Bowling Council (NBC) was created in 1943 by a coalition of manufacturers, proprietors, and leagues to promote bowling across the country.

Factory workers were also a great audience for bowling. In 1940, the Industrial Recreation Association for American

Coca-Cola was one of many companies that sponsored scoring sheets. A young couple in Clinton, Indiana, uses a grease pencil to mark up their tally in February, 1940.

Industry developed to gather ideas and techniques to advance employee recreation, to produce handbooks and manuals, to conduct conferences, and to develop the "new industrial operation called human relations." There was a massive push to get employers and factory owners to sponsor industrial leagues and compete in tournaments, partially to raise funds for charities like the Red Cross and the USO. Women embarked on a "Wings of Mercy" program that raised over $300,000 for an ambulance and three ambulance planes.

In addition, defense plants were operating around the clock. Industrial recreational programs assisted the unprecedented productivity during the war, helping keep crowds of overtaxed war workers on an even keel, and providing a respite from the monotony of work. Bowling alleys close to these plants operated on three shifts, staying open around the clock, a trend that continued long after the war ended.

Ladies' leagues greatly expanded on the homefront while so many men were overseas. The WIBC almost doubled its membership during the war. Vassar College added bowling to its intramural collegiate sports program, and the Tower Bowl in San Diego was the first bowling center to employ "all girl pinsetters." Pro bowler Glenn Alison, a star in the sport who made headlines for bowling the first "900" game, started bowling in 1939 and remembered that the "bowling business boomed because the women started bowling during World War II. Women came into the game and it got more league play since men were working and they were at home. The business increased because of the ladies. It was great." Many soldiers who first played in the service came home with a newfound love of the game. When the war ended, men and women started to bowl together in leagues for the first time. By 1946, bowling was the nation's largest competitive sport.

California was home to many military bases and a huge aeronautics economy that

BROADWAY, SAN DIEGO, CALIFORNIA—23

The Tower Bowl (1941, S. Charles Lee) dominated its block of Broadway in downtown San Diego. The massive Streamline Moderne façade was the subject of a preservation battle in the 1980s.

was in full swing during the war, which is why one of the greatest booms during this period was in Southern California. In 1936, there were only twelve bowling alleys and seventy-five lanes operating in the entire Southern California area. But by the time Los Angeles hosted the ABC for the first time in 1947, there were 166 bowling alleys and 1,800 lanes in the area.

"America will have plenty of opportunity to find fitness through recreation in the postwar world," predicted a 1945 centennial booklet published by Brunswick. "America will work harder, perhaps, in the postwar era, as it readjusts itself to the monumental changes that must follow as we win the peace and assure our victory for its time to come, but we shall play harder and oftener, as we move from war to the best of all worlds."

By 1950, bowling was on the rise and families were already starting to bowl together. In 1948, there were twenty million bowlers in the United States. But if growth was strong during the 1940s, it exploded after the introduction of the automatic pinsetter and soared into the 1950s. As bowling rose from basements to ground level and began occupying entire structures, architecture gradually caught up. Modest modernism began to creep into designs. Simple square boxes could be jazzed up with signage or neon that accented the lines of the buildings. Theater designer S. Charles Lee, who liked to say that "the show starts on the sidewalk," crafted an outrageous vertical pylon that rose eighty feet above his Tower Bowl in San Diego. This monumental moderne arc included seven balls stacked from the marquee to the sky spelling out "BOWLING." There was no doubt what this building was used for. Efforts to preserve, relocate, or salvage Lee's masterpiece were unsuccessful, and the bowl was demolished in 1986. The 1927 Highland Park Bowl in Los Angeles was restored to its original splendor in 2016 after a long stint as a rock club, but isn't America's oldest. That honor goes to the two-lane Holler House near Milwaukee, which opened in 1908 and still employs real-life pinboys!

Bowling design became bolder as the sport grew in popularity in the years leading up to 1945, but the end of the war set the stage for epic changes for every aspect of life in America, and bowling was about to take off into the jet age.

Following an award-winning restoration in 2016, the Highland Park Bowl (Pennell & Young) was reopened by the 1933 Group. The lanes first opened in 1927, making them the oldest in Los Angeles.

Automatic pinsetters, like these from AMF, enabled modern bowling centers to be operated twenty-four hours a day, without the labor of pinboys.

MORE THAN DESIGN OR CULTURE OR MEDIA, technology transformed the game of bowling in the 1950s. Every item that bowlers interacted with, from pinsetters to ball returns, and even the way they dried their hands, changed radically during the decade. A slew of innovations, combined with a new interest in styling, gave the world of bowling a major mid-century makeover that forever changed the game.

The "killer app" of bowling's greatest generation was the automatic pinsetter. Inventors struggled for decades to develop a machine that would replace pins after every ball, a device that would reliably complete this backbreaking work twenty-four hours a day, without a

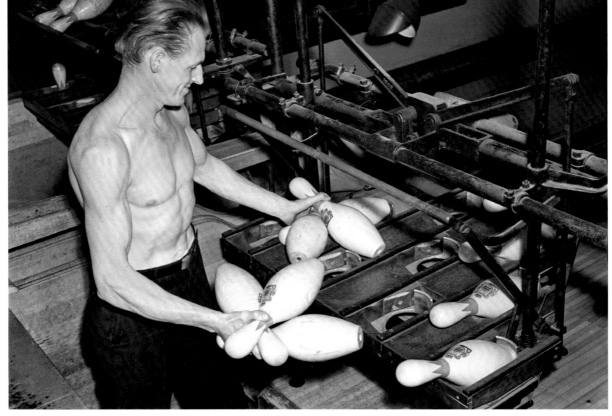

This semi-automatic B1 pinsetter by Brunswick was installed at Oregon Alleys in the 1940s. It was an innovation that made manual pinsetting a little easier for the overworked pinboy.

break, and without talking back to bowlers. Although it took years to get to market, the invention of the automatic pinsetter was as important a breakthrough to bowling as the light bulb was to Edison or the Mac was to Apple. The technology unlocked a whole new era of innovation and completely changed the way the world viewed the game.

It's hard to overstate the importance of the automatic pinsetter. Play was chaotic until 1875, when the nascent ABC adopted a regulation requiring pins to be cleared between play, and owners scrambled to find labor. Throughout history, a gang of "pinboys"

worked bowling lanes. In the nineteenth century, they started hopping down from a perch above the lanes to gather up the fallen wood after each play. Manually setting pins was a physically demanding and dangerous job due to the combination of flying pins, heavy balls, and the speed at which pinboys were expected to jump down, arrange the pins, and jump back up again. Angry customers sometimes aimed at pinboys while they were working.

Owners had trouble keeping these employees throughout the year and liked to complain about their unreliability and bad behavior. Their rowdiness became legend.

Although some players looked back fondly on the pinboy era, once the machines marched in, its days were numbered.

Proprietor Irv Noren remembered how pinboys "threw those balls as hard as they could" while returning them to the customer. A pinsetter in the 1940s said that broken limbs were not uncommon. Pinboys would taunt bowlers. They would laugh at bad male bowlers and make lewd comments to women. Sometimes they would flirt by leaving notes in the finger holes of women's balls. Since pinboys were paid per game, they would get angry if bowlers took their time. Audrey Eisenberg, the co-owner of Tropicana Lanes, remembered how uncomfortable struggling pinboys made her when she saw them while on a youthful date. "It was terrible, you had to throw money down to them," she remembers. "They were kids that needed money there in the back."

Proprietors put up with unprofessionalism and bad behavior because they didn't have a choice. Even a center filled with customers couldn't open the lanes if they didn't have pinboys working. In 1960, the editor of a Northern California newspaper described his memories of these waifs as thin and "gnome-like," and cringed at bowling alleys filled with "young hoodlums and juvenile delinquents." The Fair Labor Standards Act, which set federal standards for child labor, including minimum age requirements, didn't go into effect until 1938. During the saloon years, pinboys could be as young as seven years old. In addition to the children and teens doing this dangerous work, owners hired itinerant men, or sometimes the elderly or disabled. Many alleys had a hard time keeping enough pinboys, so they added meager lodging. One owner described these rooms as a "dorm with bunk beds." Irv Noren noted that alcoholism ran rampant. "There was a cot [for pinsetters to sleep on] with a fifth of bourbon on it." Glenn Levant, whose parents owned Reseda Bowl, agreed: "Sometimes they were difficult to wake up. You could get people to stay in the

The AMF model 82-10 automatic pinsetter created a sea change in the bowling industry when it was introduced in 1946, ending the pinboy era and bringing sophistication to the game.

A vast array of switches and gadgetry employed by the counter man at Holiday Bowl (1958, Armet & Davis) in Los Angeles. ◆ Opposite: Like the lonely Maytag repairman in those old TV commercials, a mechanic waits patiently by his reliable AMF 82-30 machines.

dormitory, but you couldn't get them to work."

For men living on the edge and in close quarters, tensions ran high. During one particularly heated fight in 1947, one L.A. pinboy killed another, striking him over the head with a tenpin. "And that's the last I can remember until I found myself on the way home on a streetcar," twenty-six-year-old Michael Burns asserted. "When I read of [fellow pinboy Edward] Browski's death in the paper, I realized I should give myself up." Witnesses told authorities Burns left the alley after a fight, demanding a gun from the proprietor, who refused to give him a weapon. Burns was reported to have gone back to the alley and "slugged it out" with heavy wooden tenpins. It wasn't all murderers and ruffians, though. Levant remembered that "there were some angels in there too." He remembered an elderly pinsetter nicknamed "Pop Rookie." "My dad told me he was an old derelict, but had been a famous thoroughbred horse trainer at Santa Anita in the '20s and '30s who wound up a pinboy."

These behaviors, combined with an unsavory, working-class atmosphere, gave the game a back alley reputation that rendered it unsuitable for women and children. Operators longed for a solution, and it came in the form of machine-operated pinsetters, underground ball returns, and major technological innovations that advanced the game and pulled bowling out of the "saloon era" and into the machine age. What if there was a machine that was more reliable and cost less per line than a pinboy's meager salary?

Fed up with pinboy shenanigans, New York proprietor George Beckerle challenged one of his customers, Gottfried Schmidt, to invent a machine to take their place. Schmidt was an engineer at the Dexter Folder company and worked across the street from the lanes. Beckerle wondered if you could lift pins with suction the way Dexter's machines did with paper. Gathering engineers in an abandoned turkey house nearby, Schmidt and company

Early Brunswick A series pinsetting machine, set with pins from the American Bowling Congress. ◆ Opposite: AMF utilized a new mascot, Mr. Pinspotter, to advertise their line of automatic pinsetters. The friendly robot showed up on matchbook covers, grand opening banners, and pencils proclaiming "No more pin-boy blues."

cobbled together a cumbersome contraption made of flower pots and lampshades and, eventually, it worked! Schmidt filed for a patent in 1936 and pitched the machine to Robert Kennedy at Brunswick. The company had tried to develop such a machine for years and had inventor Ernest Hedenskoog on the payroll since 1911. They passed on the crude apparatus. A year later, Kennedy had moved on but remembered the device. He took it to Morehead Patterson, vice president of American Machine and Foundry (AMF), most known as a manufacturer of cigarette machines.

AMF engineers took to making improvements, but the Great Depression was still grinding away, and the world soon went to war. The first postwar bowling tournament was held in Buffalo, New York, in March of 1946. AMF rented an empty garage across the street from the tournament to unveil their long-awaited invention, dubbed the Model 82-10. These proto-pinsetters were eight feet tall, filled with thousands of parts, and weighed two tons.

Some fifty thousand people crowded in to see the mechanical marvels in action on opening night. A Paramount newsreel showcased "bowling's electric brain" in action at

Left: Rayon, Dacron, Orlon and a multitude of miracle fabrics (all made of plastic) could be long-lasting, colorfast, and wrinkle free. Bowlers loved them and enthusiastically ordered all the extras including piping, deep pleats for freedom of movement, and endless customization. ◆ Right: King Louie's popular bowling shirts advertised "Color is forever."

flocking and embroidered lettering. Their color combinations were purportedly selected by star bowlers, so amateurs could dress like the pros. Air-Flo went more glitzy with the rayon "linin" Two Tone 300, offered in seven color combinations with knit sleeves and collars, strike symbols on the trim, bowling pin-shaped buttons, platinum glowing Scotchglo or sequined lettering styles, and swiss embroidery that could accommodate "all types of automotive, lodge, business and gas company emblems." Not to be outdone,

Hilton, the "aristocrat of bowling shirts," had tri-tone shirts in eight color combinations, made of Sheen-Glo gabardine and the "miracle fiber Acrilan," a jersey knit which was not only colorfast, it resisted "shrinkage, sagging, wrinkles, heat, chemicals, moths, and mildew." Today we call it polyester.

In 1962, AMF worked with European dress designers to start their own clothing line. It premiered with a fashion show at the Syosset Lanes in Long Island featuring skirts, pants, culottes, shirts, jackets, and sweaters

Introducing the incomparable new **Lady Brunswick**

in distinctive pastel blue and white

FIRST BOWLING BALL MADE JUST FOR WOMEN

In an attempt to court women in the 1950s, companies introduced new colors and styles to many products. In 1959, Brunswick introduced their "Lady Brunswick" line of balls, bags, and shoes.

from couturiers like Chanel as well as designs from Rome, Mexico City, Dublin, London, Munich, and Florence. Department stores had their own bowling lines as well. AMF ran full-color ads featuring leading social figures wearing fashionable clothes to "bring more non-bowling women onto your lanes."

Until the beginning of the twentieth century, bowling balls were typically made of lignum vitae. But the game received a big boost in 1905, when the first rubber bowling ball, the "Evertrue," was introduced. By 1914, the Brunswick Corporation was promoting their "Mineralite" ball, and touting its "mysterious rubber compound."

Fast forward to the postwar era, when chemical developments created high-performance bowling balls with new features purported to raise scores. Brunswick's popular "Black Beauty" featured a diamond-hard "Durajet finish" that was resistant to scratches and dents. The "Fireball" featured a high tech "Dyna-Core" center to adjust the bias, or curve, of the throw to hit the center.

Pins, once made entirely of hardwoods, went plastic with the promise of higher scores. AMF introduced a hybrid "Woodwelded" pin, noting that the "rich, lustrous finish bespeaks top quality." Pins were offered in "plain, fibre, or Permabase," with plastic bottoms that were American Bowling Congress-approved.

Brunswick and AMF both unveiled entirely new design collections in numerous colorways to wrap around all this technology. Brunswick called their 1958 designs in molded fiberglass the "Gold Crown" line, and AMF dubbed theirs "Streamlane" and introduced it at the 1959 ABC Tournament. AMF engineers worked in cooperation with American industrial designer Henry Dreyfuss for years developing pieces from molded thermoplastics. An all new "Magic Triangle" signaling unit and a turn-table "Magic Circle" ball return were part of the unique line. Expert styling was also brought to AMF's scoring table unit, score projector, scorer's chair, spectator seats, bowler's settees, bowling locker, "Magic Action" automatic ball cleaner and polisher, and the ball storage rack. A dimensional version of the AMF logo was part of the new look for their "Magic Triangle" Pindicator Signaling Unit mounted against a lighted background panel, creating a glowing triangle to drive home the brand identity.

Advancements in materials technology were also applied to the architecture of bowling centers themselves. In 1961, "Liquid-Applied Plastic" formed the roofing for the magnificent entrance canopy at Willow Grove Lanes. Architects created a hyperbolic paraboloid form that mimicked the shapes of thin shell concrete for the entrance canopy from 7,500 square feet of plywood over a steel frame by applying DuPont's patented synthetic rubber, called Hypalon, and covering it in liquid Neoprene. Additional chips of Neoprene were applied over the liquid to provide texture. This lightweight membrane provided waterproofing and a smooth finish over this unusual dynamic shape.

Brunswick went all out helping their sales staff promote a lavish new line of furnishings, decor, and equipment intended to update and unify interiors across the country. Even in a center that dated back decades, the new Gold Crown Line could make it as fresh as the future. The company presented

the new line in a three-hour industrial musical extravaganza at their national sales meeting in Chicago, and in a short film called *The Golden Years* in 1960.

The line was already winning awards when it was less than a week old. Among the 350 new plastic products, Brunswick's fiberglass locker room bench with ball rests took

Bowlers Journal is the oldest magazine covering the sport, and in 1961 the *Journal* introduced an annual architecture issue. Powers, Daly & DeRosa's Willow Grove Park Lanes graced the second cover in September, 1962.

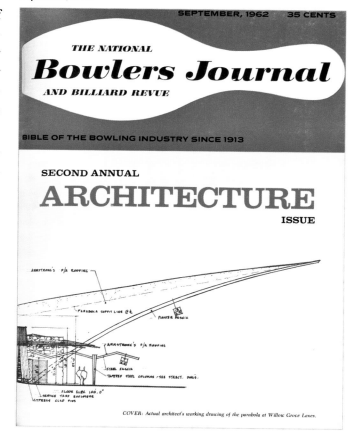

grand prize honors in the Society of the Plastic Industry's Reinforced Plastics Division judging. In the sporting goods category, the hood of the new in-line and cluster subway ball returns won first prize.

Awards by the panel of design experts were based on "originality of application or design, material selection, color, utility, moldability and appearance." Besides its completely streamlined design, the Gold Crown Line introduced custom color to bowling. Equipment was offered in any combination in six coordinated colors: Tangerine, Coral, Green, Blue, Classic White, or Gold. Remnants of the Gold Crown era can still be seen today. The odd chair, masking unit, or ball return still installed at an out-of-the-way center is a totem of bowling's glory years.

Brunswick innovated an entire suite of products throughout the 1950s that made it easier and more comfortable to bowl, but also made entering the field more attractive to prospective owners by promising a plug-and-play operation. The AMF Sparemaker featured a map to missed pins, and its lighted arrows suggested a plan for picking up that spare. Who could argue if a player went over the line when the Tel-E-Foul buzzed? A

The massive jutting roof at Willow Grove Park Lanes (1961, Powers, Daly & DeRosa) in Willow Grove, Pennsylvania, was built from steel and covered in plywood coated with flexible liquid-applied plastic roofing from Armstrong.

robot referee can't be biased. By 1962, even the tedious task of oiling the lanes could be overcome with the help of the B90 automatic oiling machine. Some owners experimented with vending machines instead of restaurants to eliminate kitchens, labor, and inventory. And all of the little extras—from cupholders on the backs of chairs waiting for a drink from the snack bar, to the coin-operated Lustre-King custom ball conditioner or Crown Imperial ball cleaner and polisher on the concourse—promised increased profits. One of the largest conglomerates in Southern California named themselves Automated Sports Centers, Inc., a promise of bowling's push-button future.

Technology continues to evolve in the modern era. In 2023, the United States Bowling Congress certified a new type of automatic pinsetter with strings attached to the pins. They were tested at the group's Texas research center using a robotic arm, dubbed the Enhanced Automated Robotic Launcher, or E.A.R.L., named for bowling great Earl Anthony. Experts say the new machines are cheaper and easier to operate, but not all players are enamored of them, citing not just the effects of strings interfering with pins and other physical forces at play, but even the different sound the clattering pins make. It might be easier to make a high score at today's most advanced lanes, but some argue that plastic pins, plastic lanes, and string machines steal some of the game's soul.

The Brunswick Gold Crown Line. Seen here: twin masking units finished in tangerine, one of six colors in the line, was the star of the 1961–1962 *Brunswick Supplies & Equipment* catalog.

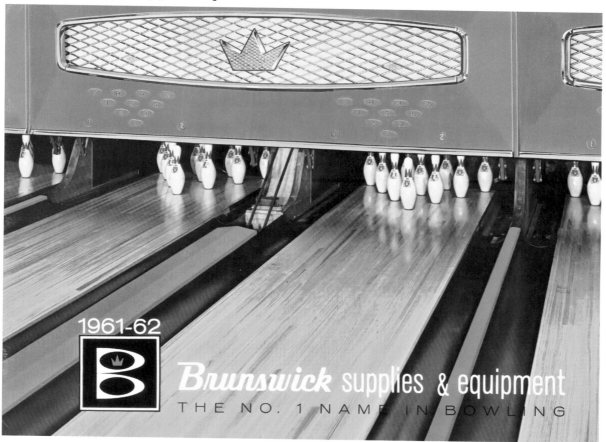

CHAPTER 3

ARCHITECTURE

Lee Linton's renderings were fantastical aspirations that Los Angeles architects Armet & Davis brought to life. Their El Rodeo Bowl opened in LA's Baldwin Hills neighborhood in 1957.

WHEN FRANK LLOYD WRIGHT WAS BORN shortly after the Civil War, an architectural revolution was just beginning. Architects were discovering new materials like steel, which allowed them to create taller buildings with broader spans—lighter and more efficient than those built of stone, brick, or wood. A few visionary architects saw the potential for an entirely new architecture that wouldn't have to repeat the historical styles that had ruled architecture for centuries. Greek, Roman, Gothic, and Renaissance styles could give way to something entirely new—Modern architecture.

As a young man, Wright had the fortune of working for one of those visionaries:

Louis Sullivan. Sullivan coined the phrase "form follows function" to express his interest in starting a design from the purpose of the building instead of repeating age-old precedents. Instead of being gussied up with historic ornament, Wright's long, simple horizontal lines were clean and effortless, and seemed to grow out of the broad Midwestern prairie landscape. Wright's designs were always close to organic nature and caught on with other architects, creating the Prairie Style.

Never one to hide his own talent, Wright published books with drawings of his buildings after the turn of the century. Idealistic architects in Europe were electrified by them; they had also been experimenting with steel, glass, and new ideas, but here were brilliant, fully-realized concepts—and they were actually being built in America and changing the world through architecture.

From Wright, many European architects saw how to break loose from the past. Utilizing steel, reinforced concrete, and glass, young architects like Ludwig Mies van der Rohe, Walter Gropius, Le Corbusier, and other early adopters of Modernism learned how to change the look of cities from piles of neoclassical brick and stone to glass and steel boxes.

Many young European architects, learning of these advances in America, yearned to work there—especially after World War I decimated many of Europe's cities and economies. Two Viennese schoolmates, Rudolph

Schindler and Richard Neutra, especially wanted to work with Frank Lloyd Wright. Schindler immigrated first, in 1914, working with Wright in Wisconsin and then moving to Los Angeles to supervise the landmark Hollyhock House. After stops in Chicago and with Wright at Taliesin after the war, Neutra also found his way to Los Angeles. This booming city being reshaped by the automobiles Americans were buying in droves already looked like the future to him.

Neutra and Schindler would become two of the most influential Modernist architects

Concept for Plaza Lanes (1960) in Long Beach by architect Kenneth Wing for the Alamitos Land Company. Wing also designed the nearby Circle Bowl (1957) and Belmont Bowl (1947).

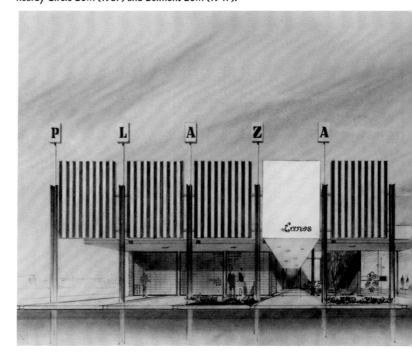

The biomorphic façade for the Bowl-O-Drome (1957, Arthur Froehlich) in Torrance, California, precedes the architect's work designing Belmont Park and Hollywood Park racetracks and the Hanna-Barbera cartoon studio in Hollywood.

modern concrete construction.

Modernism continued to inspire new ideas, forms, and materials. By the 1930s, the pendulum swung toward more spartan forms that came to be known as Streamline Moderne. An aerodynamic style that signaled a sense of speed by using horizontal lines, rounded corners, and luminescent glass blocks, it was inspired by contemporaneous advances in steamships, airplanes, and railroads. Two titans of industrial design, Raymond Loewy and Donald Deskey, helped introduce these dynamic, unadorned forms. Experiment was always at the root of Modern architecture, and Brunswick hired Donald Deskey to bring his modern ideas to bowling.

John Lautner was a student of Wright who came to Los Angeles in the 1940s and practiced a brand of Modernism that would eventually yield sculptural masterpieces of concrete and steel, but early in his career he designed restaurants and commercial buildings. His Googies restaurant on the Sunset Strip lent its name to a whole new architectural genre. Googie restaurants featured bold shapes and large signs to catch the eye of passing drivers, and open dining rooms with huge windows where customers could see and be seen. The style evolved through the firm of Armet & Davis, which utilized new materials like fiberglass and formica, an abundance of natural stone, and otherworldly landscaping.

These designs juxtaposed natural materials like wood and stone with precise and

of the twentieth century. Their work was startling at the time, though it became a standard approach to Modern design. In both America and Europe, the emerging, evolving Modern architecture generated a variety of shapes, forms, and spaces rendered in steel, concrete, and wood as technology improved these materials and architects imagined new ways to utilize them. At the same time that Schindler and Neutra generally eschewed ornament (letting their materials and geometries provide visual interest), Wright drew on both organic shapes and pre-Columbian designs—but adapted to

The Safari Room lounge at Plaza Lanes (1960, architect unknown) in San Jose, California, became renowned for live music. The roof of the restaurant reaches down into the landscape. ◆ Opposite: A bold sawtooth roof protects the Picnic coffee shop fronting the Holiday Bowl (1958, Armet & Davis) in Los Angeles's Crenshaw neighborhood.

unusual geometry that doesn't occur in nature. The composition was set in a fantasy landscape that often mixed tropical and desert plants, an otherworldly combination of species that had no business being neighbors. Spiky palms and yuccas followed the jaunty angles of the building, and as humorist Charles Phoenix puts it, "[Burst] out of the ground like the Fourth of July."

Accenting that composition with futuristic signage, fixtures and details created a tension between the primitive and the modern, bristling with energy that launched these confections into the stratosphere. The Egyptian-themed Covina Bowl incorporated palms, tree ferns, and philodendrons into their "soft desert" landscape, even adding a small sand dune under the entrance pyramid. Planting so-called "soft desert" and luxuriant shade gardens next to each other only enhanced the contrast.

Stone pillars, walls, and planters crafted from locally mined boulders welcomed visitors. The rough and rustic organic material was supremely durable and looked as if it rose out of the earth. The character of each stratified stone was brought out by creative placement in walls and in the landscape by craftsmen seeking to showcase the natural history that evolved from centuries of weathering. The master mason of Covina Bowl was Giuseppe (Joe) Mascarin, who hand-placed one hundred tons of Bouquet Canyon stone there. Mascarin had become a skilled artisan in his native Italy where trades were often passed from father to son.

Once lured to the endless acres of free parking, a pedestrian's view might shift to the texture of materials, such as stone and stucco and tile, only occasionally punctuated by windows or sunscreens. Next to the roofline and sign, the most prominent feature of many googie bowling centers would be the coffee shop, often placed right up front. Architects Armet & Davis stated that their goal was to design the entire center around a casual restaurant. Their designs placed the coffee shop on a prominent corner of the building where it might have transparent walls of floor-to-ceiling glass in aluminum frames to showcase the activity within. However, the lanes, lounge, and the treasures inside were strictly opaque. "The guys who have never been in a bowling center. They inevitably design a building with huge windows," architect Pat B. DeRosa remembered. "The glare, especially if the window faces west, makes the place practically useless during the day. At night, they have to contend with the lights from passing cars. Windows do not belong in bowling centers, except in special applications. Non-glare glass on side entrances, for example, is fine." Some windows sported grille work that assisted air conditioning in keeping interiors temperate.

Googie bowling centers were party up front and business in the back. Even the most elaborate designs kept the exterior razzle dazzle contained to a primary façade, with the bulk of the building composed of concrete block or tilt-up concrete. Contractors had been speeding up construction by pouring concrete into a form on the ground and lifting it into place as early as 1908, when the technique was utilized by Thomas Edison, but it didn't gain popularity until the easy availability of ready-mix concrete and mobile cranes after World War II. Both techniques rapidly gained popularity during the 1950s building boom.

Pioneering educator Ann Darling already had a school, shopping center, and housing project named after her in San Jose, California, when the Ann Darling Bowl (architect unknown) was completed in 1959.

Left: Victory Lanes (1948, architect unknown) in Pacific Beach, San Diego, California, combined Streamline Moderne curves with neon tubing outlining a transparent, modern building. ◆ Right: A superb example of "building as sign," the Pomona Recreation Center (1948, Sidney W. Orme) in Pomona, California, glowed under miles of exposed neon.

"Tilt up is a great way to go," remembered Covina Bowl architect Gordon Powers. "It's a lot cheaper and it's really fast." A criticism of these buildings is that they are decorated boxes with all the pizazz on the front.

Some communities, at the urging of religious organizations that considered a sign, window, or door for a cocktail lounge a moral hazard, dictated solid walls with no signage. Elsewhere, signs did the heavy lifting. Towers of steel wrapped in glass tubes charged with neon fronted nearly every center. Balls, arrows, and every form of geometry manifested in bright lights, glowing plastic, and animation. Signs grew so large they could be seen from blocks away, which was the entire point. Like some kind of sci-fi monster glowing and crowing, massive neon signs demanded dominance and ate up the landscape. It's no

wonder there was a backlash that made them nearly extinct just a few years later.

King Louie West Lanes in Overland Park, Kansas, opened in 1959 with a sloping folded plate roof whose rafters ended in a series of triangular stone buttresses buried in the ground. The undulating form was intended to "hide the mass of what was under it," according to architect Manuel Morris. Some have compared the building to Taliesin West and the Marin County Civic Center. "There was definitely a Frank Lloyd Wright influence," Morris said. "In shapes, materials and the metal and stone spire at the entrance."

Architects inspired by the organic philosophy of Frank Lloyd Wright abound, and many of the best designers share a lineage with the greats of modern architecture. Some of the biggest names in architecture dipped

Some of the best and brightest Los Angeles architects tried their hand at designing bowling centers during the 1950s. Top row from left: Eldon Davis and Louis Armet, A. Quincy Jones, Ed Killingsworth. Bottom row, from left: Paul R. Williams, Dike Nagano, Martin Stern Jr., Helen Fong. ◆ Opposite: Pink and gold neon dances over the chrome and glass of this couple's car as they prepare for an evening at Covina Bowl (1956, Powers, Daly & DeRosa).

their toes in the pool of bowling design, including some of those behind the legendary *Arts & Architecture* Case Study House program, the USC School of Architecture, and the first Black and Korean architects in California. Names that are once removed from more famous names like Frank Lloyd Wright and Mies van der Rohe, but who incorporated similar ideas into their work. The flashiest flash was brought by Los Angeles's most famous movie theater designer S. Charles Lee

and the kingpins of the Googie coffee shop, Armet & Davis, who just cranked the design up to eleven.

It wasn't that critics at the time were unkind; they were completely oblivious to bowling centers and generally blind to commercial architecture in general. Looking back, we might find a fine print reference to a motel or a restaurant in the architectural journals, but the avant garde modern designs from firms like Armet & Davis or Powers, Daly, & DeRosa

were largely ignored. Even the leading magazine of the industry, *Bowlers Journal*, rarely discussed design until 1961, when it suddenly began devoting entire issues to it. Local newspapers did their best to acknowledge the strange new forms rising at the edge of town, like when the *Oakland Tribune* praised the "ultra-contemporary" and "dynamic" Walnut Bowl shortly before it opened in California's Contra Costa County. "The design," the paper noted, "should win awards." However, the folks that give architecture awards are not often seen in bowling alleys. In 1961, San Fernando Valley architectural firm Johnson, Ensen & D'Agostino designed Pickwick Bowl in Burbank, and an entire tract of hillside homes overlooking the Valley. The house designs won a "Home of the Year" award from *Good Housekeeping*. The bowling center won nothing. "Critics hated this populist, roadside commercial California architecture," says architectural historian Alan Hess.

The *New York Times* described the essayist Russell Lynes as "one of America's foremost arbiters of taste." Lynes favored bow ties, pipe smoking, and Bugatti cars and wrote

Flames shot from the tops of these eighty-foot masts at Five Points Bowl (1958, Johnson & Engen) in El Monte, California. ◆ Opposite: The owners of Bel Mateo Bowl (1957, Powers, Daly & DeRosa) in San Mateo, California, were inspired by the legendary hospitality of the Haida tribe in British Columbia. Their Totem Room included modernist interpretations of indigenous art, and an abstract steel totem pole still adorns a water feature at the entrance.

Chicago architect Richard Barancik "just wanted to do something that would be eye-catching" when he created the 1959 Orchard Twin Bowl in Skokie, Illinois. "Did I have a sense of adventure?" he retorted. "Yes."

extensively on American culture. His books of the 1940s and 1950s included *Highbrow, Lowbrow, Middlebrow, Snobs*, and *The Tastemakers*. In 1963, Lynes held his nose long enough to visit America's largest bowling center for an essay in *Horizon* magazine. The critic compared the vast opulence to razzle-dazzle jazz age movie palaces with the kineticism of pinball machines. He chides the size of the rocks on the fieldstone exterior, the Wrightian wood detailing, and even the colored exterior floodlights. He didn't miss a chance to get in a jab at the king of New Formalism, describing a screen block wall as "Edward Durrell Stone piled on Edward Durrell Stone." His ignorance of the genre led to him relegating it to second class status, writing it off as belonging to "that family of flat-chested but muscular rococo to which a great many motels and shopping centers also belong."

Lynes describes bowling centers as "public palaces" and compares their mass appeal to "opry" houses and the tawdry entertainment on Mississippi riverboats a century earlier. Those lumbering barges were often filled with clowns and minstrels and show people. Kids on shore would paddle out hoping that frolickers would toss coins to them. He invokes Mark Twain's take on the boats, "they tallied with the citizen's dream of what magnificence was, and satisfied it," to understand the reasoning behind a palace for the people.

The opulence could be a little over the top. Flaming torches atop eighty-foot masts in El Monte, fountains and pools flanking the entrance of Willow Grove Park Lanes, and twenty-four-carat, gold-plated automatic doors at the entrance of Cotton Bowling Palace near Dallas. Perhaps that's what the *Times* meant when describing Lynes's amusement

Top: Stone columns growing out of a jungle landscape support outrigger beams atop the coffee shop at Stardust Bowl (1960, Armet & Davis) in West Covina, California. ◆ Bottom: An epic screen block wall outside of Kapu Kai in Cucamonga (1962, Talley-Guevara Associates) laid in the "Satel-Lite" pattern.

with "stuffed shirts with more money than taste and unstuffed shirts who spent what little they had on vulgar design and overstated ornamentation."

A dramatic wood laminated arch soaring over the entrance to Orchard Twin Bowl near Chicago was dreamed up by architect Richard Barancik in 1961. Barancik enrolled in the University of Cambridge shortly after his service in World War II, when the soldier was a crucial part of the Monuments, Fine Arts, and Archives division, known as the Monuments Men, tasked with recovering the world's looted art treasures from the Nazis. While he was studying at the École des Beaux-Arts in Paris, he paid a visit to one of his heroes, Le Corbusier. He left disappointed. "He always talked about cleanliness and his office was filthy," he remembered. "He had an old roll top desk with a faded picture of the Parthenon above it." He left an evening with his hero Frank Lloyd Wright similarly nonplussed. "He invited me up to Taliesin in Spring Green, Wisconsin," Barancik remembered recently. "On Saturday night he would sit on the dais and his students would come and kneel in front of him and he'd tell them what he thought of each project. He asked me, 'What do you think of my chicks,' and I said, 'I think you sat on the eggs too long.' [Wright's son-in-law] William Wesley Peters whispered in my ear, 'Mr. Wright would like you to get the hell out.'"

The brilliant and bristly designer ("I'm

Country Club Lanes

Watt Avenue near El Camino
Sacramento, California

The enormous, eye-catching roofline of Country Club Lanes (1960, Powers, Daly, & DeRosa) in Sacramento appears to float like a fantastic spaceship above a sea of pastel-colored cars, strategically drawing the eye to a neon sign at the entrance.

not very verbal and had a low tolerance for bullshit") split his time between Chicago and California, where he found the Golden State's roadside architecture "fun and wonderfully amusing." When asked if his midwestern designs were inspired by those he saw on the West Coast, he replied, "I think everybody is influenced by something. You just don't get an idea without something in your memory banks. I just wanted to do something that would be eye-catching." After more prodding about how such a sober designer incorporated

such a bold statement he acknowledged. "Did I have a sense of adventure? Yes. Some of my buildings were whimsical. Aesthetics were very important to me. I don't think I've ever done a building I hate."

Barancik commissioned site-specific artworks for his centers. The sculptor Abbott Pattinson created a precast concrete freeform work that was poured on the ground and lifted into place. A porcelain enamel frieze by the same artist still exists above the entrance of Barancik's Willa Cather School in Chicago.

"When I started college in the architecture school, half your courses were art courses," says the art-loving architect, who helped save five million artworks seized by Hitler and hidden in castles and salt mines. "Because architects had to draw and had to have a background in the history of architecture." He even drew his own renderings until the firm grew too large.

From the graphics on menus and matchbooks to custom artwork created to reflect the theme of each location, Armet & Davis liked their restaurants to tell a story and transport customers someplace special. The coffee shops they designed were often inexpensive and open all night. They were more likely to be found in the new suburbs rather than in the city center, although Armet & Davis famously wedged an exuberant googie roof into the ground floor of a downtown hotel. If they added a bar (excuse me—a cocktail lounge) it would allow visitors a chance to slip out of the stuffy formality of modernism and into something more comfortable. Themes with catchy names prevailed, and artwork, décor, and low lighting transformed even the most modest booze rooms into a pirate galleon or a tiki temple.

Armet & Davis, along with other prominent firms of the era, brought the luxurious, exuberant googie style to bowling centers in the 1950s, creating iconic masterpieces and transforming every aspect of the mid-century bowling experience. Why shouldn't a fun center be joyful and exuberant? The best of them combine a cool modernism with warm, organic elements to create something new and wonderful. Some observers might find ambitious steel and glass modernism cold, and bringing it back to earth with stone and plants warms it up. Compare Richard Neutra to Frank Lloyd Wright.

The best mid-century bowling centers are big and loud. They're not uncouth, they're just doing their job. The shapes are in-your-face, but refined. The visual tension and sense of movement can bring the composition to life, and the crown of an animated neon sign can activate that motion with sparkling electricity. This architecture exists to draw in customers and it's a lot of fun. That is its function, and the form accomplishes that. The arresting forms exist to break the monotony of the highway with a different rhythm that's all their own. "Fantasy can lord it over function in Southern California," critic Reyner Banham opines in *Los Angeles: The Architecture of Four Ecologies*. "The building and the symbol are one and the same."

Bold geometric shapes reaching for the sky were employed to mark the entrances of the new bowling centers, the most lavish of which were dubbed "California style" and inspired designs nationwide. Their towering peaks were surpassed only by signs stretching even higher. A survey of shapes employed for eye-catching rooflines would include the folded plate, the butterfly, the A-Frame, and

Southern California architects Pat B. DeRosa, Austin Daly, and Gordon Powers pose with a model of their Anaheim Bowl (1959). ◆ Opposite: Families leaving Friendly Hills Bowl (1957, Powers, Daly & DeRosa) cross under the butterfly roof of the porte cochere. The building was restored as an Aldi supermarket in 2016.

the hyperbolic paraboloid. Space age design is one of the hallmarks of *The Jetsons*, but California's roadside architecture inspired the show, not the other way around. "You could drive out to certain areas and see this modern architecture and we would get influenced," remembers animator Willie Ito. "Bowling centers or drive-in theaters and restaurants were all very futuristic to me with that modern architecture. Living in Los Angeles did give us a lot of good ideas." The Milky Way Bowling Center, seen in the 1962

episode "A Visit From Grandpa," had all the googie: flashy signs as big as the building, balls orbiting a giant pin on the roof, and a series of elegant thin shells that tapered to a fine point. All that plus abundant free parking and it was open all night! Ito's colleagues at Hanna-Barbera, who bowled together on a team called the Yogi Bears, worked the game into *The Flintstones*, *Huckleberry Hound*, and many of their iconic cartoons.

The kingpins of the mid-century "California-style" bowling center were

The gloriously googie Covina Bowl (1956, Powers, Daly & DeRosa), shortly after it was completed in 1956, was an instant landmark in the new suburbs.

architects Gordon F. Powers, Austin W. Daly & Pasquale "Pat" B. DeRosa of Long Beach, California. Most of the bowling center architects were little known outside of their field, but the firm Powers, Daly & DeRosa became the absolute masters of the form, reinventing the industry, and spreading California dreaming from coast to coast with their portfolio of more than seventy bowling centers built during a bowling boom that lasted less than a decade. The firm was organized in 1953 and created shopping centers, medical buildings, and churches before pivoting to bowling. They designed at least seventy-two centers, including the world's largest, Willow Grove Park Lanes in Willow Grove, Pennsylvania. Powers was the businessman who landed the jobs, Daly had incredible planning and technical skills, and DeRosa dreamed up fantastical designs.

Their masterpiece, Covina Bowl, set the standard for the googie bowling center and thrust their firm into prominence, establishing them as the leaders in the field. Covina Bowl was eons ahead of anything bowlers had ever seen, and it was plunked down in the middle of nowhere: Covina, California. The town was rapidly evolving from an orange grove to a bedroom community, and, without a freeway, it was a good hour from Los Angeles. Covina Bowl pioneered features that would become commonplace in bowling centers. Let's start

Java Lanes (1958, Powers, Daly & DeRosa) was one of the architects' most prominent works. The cavernous entrance to the East Indies Room and corkscrew sign fit right into the roadside strip.

with the theme. A modernist take on ancient Egypt, the structure features a massive soaring pyramid at the entrance that sets the tone for the whole compound. Add an oversized neon sign, straight out of Las Vegas, bursting through a zigzag porte cochere with stone columns—but you haven't even made it to the front door yet. One hundred tons of Bouquet Canyon stone rise out of the same desert-meets-jungle landscaping we'd see at a googie coffee shop. A terrazzo concourse that would, by 1962, stretch to fifty lanes featured a coffee shop, the Pyramid Room nightclub, myriad banquet rooms, a billiards parlor, and a supervised children's playroom opposite the bowling lanes. Additional commercial space tucked into the landscape would ultimately include a beauty parlor, Radio Shack, and offices for bowling groups.

The firm was suddenly thrust into the spotlight after the success of Covina Bowl. "Proprietors from Passaic to Portland began to pour down the San Bernardino Freeway," gushed the *Bowlers Journal*, "to see the nonconformist darling of bowling architecture, which had been built in a nondescript little suburb, some twenty-five miles east of downtown Los Angeles." Powers, Daly & DeRosa started taking clients on road trips to the San Gabriel Valley to drum up new business.

The three men couldn't have been more different. Pat DeRosa was born in Brooklyn and lived in the tenements, where he played stickball with the other neighborhood

Top: An admirer stands in front of the newly completed Fairfield Bowl (1958, Powers, Daly & DeRosa) in Fairfield, California. ◆ Bottom: A pair of concrete domes mark the entrance to Futurama Lanes (1958, Powers, Daly & DeRosa) in San Jose, California.

children. "Growing up with other kids from various immigrant families taught me appreciation for the different and interesting customs of each," he said in 1965. DeRosa won an architecture scholarship and graduated from the Pratt Institute and, after army service, relocated to the West Coast and joined the firm in 1955. DeRosa had an outsized personality: a jazz musician who "cooked" with his band (they performed a gig with the Herb Giffords combo at Java Lanes in 1958) as well as in the kitchen. He beamed when the local newspaper ran his Italian omelet recipe next to a photo of him in a chef's hat. When the Long Beach University Club threw a "suppressed desires" party, DeRosa and his wife dressed

as a big game hunter and "wild jungle girl."

His partner Gordon Powers was a hunter in real life, continuing to take out his hounds

well into his nineties. He was an ex-military man who kept a rigorous posture but was quick with a funny aside. On one of his last visits to Covina Bowl, he flashed a toothy grin and kept a sparkle in his eye as he barked out orders to the manager to go create a league from shoppers at the nearby Home Depot.

"Austin [Daly] always had a big office and always smelled like a cigar. He was quite a character," says Arron F. Latt, who designed supermarkets, banks, and retail stores with Austin Daly after he left Powers, Daly & DeRosa. "They were the bowling alley kings of the western world." Latt loved working with Daly because clients enjoyed the character he gave to industrial buildings, which were basically big boxes with holes in them.

A collection of Architectural Pottery by ceramicist LaGardo Tackett adorns the garden at the entrance to the restaurant at 300 Bowl (1958, Powers, Daly & DeRosa) in Phoenix, Arizona. This space age spectacle still soars over Phoenix, and represents googie architecture at its dramatic best.

Daly's work helped to "legitimize our architectural end of the business," Latt says.

While all three designers contributed to the success of the firm, it was DeRosa's imagination that ran to the farthest corners of outer space. "The forms were free-form . . . the more startling the better," DeRosa said in 1986. "I just dreamed about them. Everyone was space conscious. The more forms you used the better, especially if [the building] looked like it was just floating there, if you couldn't see how it could stand up. That was the trick of it."

DeRosa's daughter Nina remembers her dad's fascination with the folded shapes and graceful movement of kites and his love of the stars. After his family gifted him a telescope for their desert home, he renamed his design company for the constellation Orion.

Most googie architects focused their attention on big, bold shapes that could be seen from blocks away. If you could stretch that shape all the way to the roof, that strong shape can act like a second sign. Some of the best could echo the theme of the whole project, as in the pyramid at Covina Bowl; some provided shelter for visitors by acting as a porte cochere. The roofline's most important function, once it made you pull over, was directing you to the front door. The rhythm of shape, color, and form along the roadside was meant to be read through the windshield. It was to be viewed at thirty-five miles per hour while cruising by in your land yacht, neon dancing over chrome and glass.

Starting in the late 1950s, California's best and brightest architects lined up to try their hand at designing a bowling center, with mixed results. Like Richard Neutra, who made a lone attempt at crafting a gas station, many of the biggest names of mid-century California architecture, including A. Quincy Jones; Paul R. Williams; Welton Becket; Ed Killingsworth; Stiles O. Clements; Kenneth Wing; Dike Nagano; Daniel, Mann, Johnson and Mendenhall; and Smith & Williams, seem to have given up after a few efforts to crack the bowling code.

There is a possibly apocryphal story about a client taking their architect to Ships Coffee Shop in Los Angeles to show them the look they wanted. Martin Stern, Jr., who designed two of these legendary googie landmarks, only designed one bowling center. It's hard to imagine that the outrageous cheesehole boomerang roof handle on his Sepulveda Bowl in Mission Hills didn't inspire Barney's Bowlarama on *The Simpsons*, helping to cement America's memory of what a bowling alley looks like.

The third Ships Coffee Shop was designed by Armet & Davis, the undisputed kings of googie, who designed thousands of restaurants that spread the style nationwide. The firm, founded by Louis Armet and Eldon Davis in 1947, is still going strong today. Armet Davis Newlove, as they are now known, completed at least six bowling centers in the Golden

The dynamic roofline of the Parkway Bowl (1961, Tucker, Sadler, and Bennett) looms over the fountains and landscape at the El Cajon, California, center.

Folded planes and dynamic shapes mark the entrance to Kingpin Lanes (1961, Arthur Froehlich) in Los Angeles. Multicolored diamonds in a harlequin pattern recall the theme of the Jester Room lounge inside.

State. Half of them were outfitted with a Polynesian theme in the cocktail lounge, which continued outdoors; Stardust Bowl in West Covina featured pineapple-shaped modernist lamps and outrigger beams, and Mar Vista Bowl welcomed visitors with a bamboo-and-grass-thatch entrance flanked by gas torches.

At their 1962 Delta Bowl in Antioch, Eldon Davis and Louis Armet shifted all the focus onto the coffee shop, placing it front and center. They declared that the transparent walls and stone columns that dominated the primary view in this new concept, the *raison d'etre*, for the entire structure. "The bowling section is made secondary to the café," a reporter noted at the time.

Their Holiday Bowl was declared a Historic-Cultural Monument in the city of Los Angeles in 2000. The coffee shop portion, with its open glass walls and sawtooth roof finished with Japanese-inspired rafter tails, was restored by Starbucks, and includes public art that pays homage to the role of the bowl as a community center.

Movie palaces designed by S. Charles Lee transitioned into bowling lanes as television began to dominate over films during the 1950s. This was a trend all over the country, when fads like 3-D and Cinerama failed to bring back moviegoers who were at home leaving it to Beaver and in love with Lucy. At least once, Lee tried his hand at a bowling palace, creating the magnificent Tower Bowl in San Diego in 1941. Instead of a flashing theater marquee, Lee fashioned a tower of massive bowling balls spinning next to a streamline pylon soaring eighty feet into the sky. The venue featured all-girl pinsetters during World War II, and plenty of spectator seating. A tropical bar inside was called the Kapa Shell Room and could accommodate four hundred swing dancers. Preservation efforts failed, and his elaborate confection was demolished in 1986.

Case Study House architect Edward Killingsworth crafted two crisp and precise bowling boxes in his hometown of Long Beach, but his cool precision lacked the passion of the Powers, Daly & DeRosa designs. Racetrack specialist Arthur Froehlich was closer to the action with his jaunty butterfly-roofed Kingpin Lanes in West Los Angeles. His

A massive porte cochere decorated with bold graphics distinguished the inviting entrance to this Bowlero location in Lemon Grove (1959, Paderewski, Mitchell, and Dean), outside of San Diego, California in June 1961.

Bowl-O-Drome in Torrance, which sported a bar called the "Fun Room," was fairly sober. The best review went so far as to call it "handsome." Owners hinted at more excitement inside than out, when their opening day ad promised "When we open our doors—you will open your eyes!"

Another prominent architect, Robert Cleveland, designed film sets after graduating from the University of Washington and attending ArtCenter School in Los Angeles. He later went to work for famed industrial designer Raymond Loewy. He and partner Sterling Leach became known for their giant supermarkets and shopping centers, built at a time when "stores were putting money into graphics and color and good materials, things people will enjoy when they're shopping," says their former designer Jim Van Schaack, who had studied automotive design at ArtCenter under Sterling Leach, and appreciated the firm's connection to Loewy. Leach and Cleveland followed that ethos at their bowling projects by commissioning a mammoth mosaic for their El Dorado Lanes in Westchester and building out a pirate-themed bar called the Jolly Roger at their Granada Lanes in the San Fernando Valley.

Experiments with prefabricated plywood roof and wall systems, water-based radiant floor heating, and glass elevators made Clarence Joseph "Pat" Paderewski one of San Diego's most innovative architects of the 1950s. The UC Berkeley grad won national design competitions and taught architecture while writing about and photographing buildings for the local newspapers. His firm, Paderewski, Mitchell, and Dean, designed the 1957 Bowlero in Mission Valley, which was briefly America's largest center, and drew in customers from all around San Diego. The exterior was lit by diamond-shaped shields and featured a monumental polychrome porte cochere finished with bold graphic patterns that reflected his great interest in bringing more color to architecture, especially in his school designs. Bowlero was owned by Bill and Jack Skirball, who had produced films for Alfred Hitchcock and Bob Hope. Their 1938 film *Birth of a Baby* was famously banned for showing scenes of actual childbirth. The Skirballs owned movie theaters and resort hotels and, later in life, rabbi Jack Skirball helped fund a well-known Jewish community center in Los Angeles. They hired Paderewski to design a second Bowlero in nearby Lemon Grove two years later.

Architect Goodwin Steinberg designed tilt-up concrete centers with an exposed roof truss system for Mel's Palm Bowl in San Jose, one of four centers he designed for Mel's Drive-In owner Mel Weiss. Steinberg, who studied at the School of Fine Arts at Fontainebleau and under Bauhaus master Mies van der Rohe, noted that the trusses "were to be painted different colors with light diffusing through the members weaving into a geometry that worked with the spacing of the bowling lanes." Little of his commercial work survives, but following a historic review of his Mel's Bowl in Redwood City, the original neon sign was restored and relocated to a new site nearby along El Camino Real. Architectural historian Alan Hess described signs as "urban jewelry," and some have been retained for their historic and aesthetic value. Developers demolished Futurama Lanes in San Jose, but retained its massive pylon sign, swapping out "Futurama" for "Safeway" to suit the new supermarket built on the land. "BOWL" became "SHOP" in an adaptive reuse of Friendly Hills Lanes in Whittier.

Architecture critic Thomas Hine writes in his book *Populuxe* that "[Eero] Saarinen

Futurama Lanes in San Jose, California (1958, Powers, Daly & DeRosa). After the demolition of the bowling center, the original atomic age sign was adaptively reused and preserved in its original location. The "Futurama" portion now reads "Safeway."

ARCHITECTURE

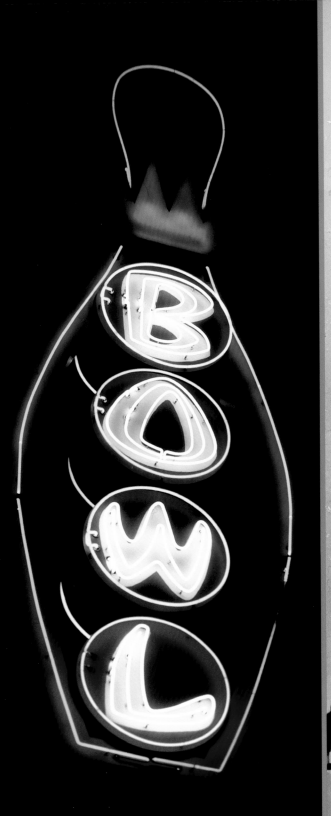

A high bar overlooks the lanes at this California bowling center captured for *Life* magazine in 1958. ◆ Opposite: A colorful dining area inside Shatto Lanes (1962, Hawkins & Lindsey) in Los Angeles is separated from the bowling lanes with concrete screen block.

The *maître d'* at the elegant Steak Knife restaurant would deliver a menu as sumptuous as the banquettes, filled with specialties like "French hors *d'oeuvres*," and luxe seafood specialties like swordfish and oysters.

Developer Joseph Eichler also sought out Jones when he wanted to build his namesake modernist housing tracts that prioritized innovative architecture and availability to all. Eichler worked to integrate neighborhoods and fought anti-discrimination laws. One of his clients was Stephen Nakashima, an attorney in San Jose who had been confined in an internment camp during World War II. "Our first house was an Eichler," his son Lex remembers. "They would sell to anyone. In the late '50s it wasn't a great time to be non-white. Eichlers were made to be affordable to anyone."

When Nakashima decided to build his own bowling center, Saratoga Lanes, in San Jose, he turned to architect Goodwin Steinberg. Many centers advertised themselves as the "Country Club of the People," riding that wave of 1950s popular luxury. The same unprecedented wave of economic prosperity during the 1950s, which brought Americans to indulgences like jet travel or a second car in the driveway, allowed them to feel like their suburban salaries afforded them membership in a country club.

Meanwhile, in Chicago, architect Richard Barancik was incorporating "sculpture, walnut, paneling, and wall-to-wall carpeting just about everywhere, except on the lanes," noted *Bowler's Journal* in 1961. The magazine declared that his Mage's Bowlarena in River Grove, Illinois, had created the "aura of a community meeting place by employing the devices of the atmosphere of a private club." The magazine goes on to outline Barancik's ultramodern designs for a "community showplace," featuring a multi-level lobby flanked by escalators and lined with gold and bronze Italian glass tile. The stairs had laminated teakwood railings in a "Swedish" design, and a "black-and-orange leaf

Teens gather to enjoy the fun and flair of 'round the clock, air-conditioned bowling in AMF's ultramodern "streamlane" environment. ◆ Opposite: Tapa cloth, thatch, and Japanese fishing floats bring the tropics to the suburbs at the Kona Kove bar inside Stardust Bowl (1960, Armet & Davis) in West Covina, California.

light ceiling." A slate-floored concourse led to the bowling lanes.

Pro bowler Don Scott designed his own interiors and went so far as to create his own design firm, Don Scott Interiors, which offered furnishing and decorating services to the competition. Scott and his wife, Vel, bought their own bowling center in Cleveland during the 1960s and gave it a modern makeover. "During the height of bowling there was a place called Alhambra Lanes," Mrs. Scott

says. "We changed it to University Lanes when we took over. You could have dinner and drinks and we had a stage. There were red upholstered booths and we could seat five hundred people in a nightclub setting."

Innovations came from owners who also enjoyed the sport. Java Lanes in Long Beach had an "unusually roomy concourse," owner Henry Cox noted in 1958. "A good number of the features we are introducing in Java Lanes are the direct result of the experiences we

have had as bowlers." Owners would express their personal taste through décor and theming. Cox's daughter, Nancy Cox Castro, remembers "my dad started by building homes and he really loved that tiki theme. There's a whole area of his homes in Garden Grove with Hawaiian names on the streets. He just loved the Polynesian stuff." Cox's Java Lanes and Kona Lanes are two of the best-remembered Polynesian Pop bowling centers. "He was a phenomenal architect," Nancy Cox Castro says. "But because he didn't have the education he called himself a draftsman."

Innovations continued to improve the atmosphere. Many alleys added a sawtooth-pattern acoustical ceiling over the lanes, which lowered the volume in the room. Some were covered with Curon, a new soundproofing material developed by aerospace company Curtiss-Wright. Advertising promised it could quiet crowd noises "yet lets you hear the 'satisfying smash' of strike." Other developments, such as adding massive spans between support columns, offered unimpeded views of the endless rows of lanes. Steel girders that could span 125 feet each were beginning to be used. They opened the vast room visually and fully exploited new developments in prefabricated trusses and open span roofing systems. At Willow Grove Park Lanes, the roof was three times the length of a football field.

The massive Willow Grove Park Lanes near Philadelphia was over 120,000 feet of fun, with four dining and drinking venues inside. It featured a soda bar called The Hutch, a hamburger and hot dog joint popular with teens, a German-themed Hofbrau delicatessen, a Tiki Room, and the Waterfall. Mitchell Hankin, whose father helped build the bowl, says his family was particularly fond of the Waterfall, a destination restaurant whose menu included specialties like Flounder Veronique and

Primitive meets modern inside the coffee shop at Stardust Bowl (1960, Armet & Davis) in West Covina, California.

White tablecloth service under flagstone walls inside the East Indies room at Java Lanes (1958, Powers, Daly & DeRosa) in Long Beach, California.

Chateaubriand for two.

Slate, terrazzo, boulders, and many kinds of stone found their way onto the designer's palette inside and out. Powers, Daly & DeRosa loved the material for its warmth and durability and worked it into walls, planters, flooring, anywhere it would fit. "We feel that the natural materials, preferably those which are native to the area, are more attractive than plaster and paint," DeRosa told *Bowler's Journal*. DeRosa noted that owners really appreciated the indestructible nature of desert boulders and the lack of required maintenance. He specified Valley Forge granite and Albany Quartz for Willow Grove and Bouquet Canyon rock for Covina Bowl. More than 320 tons of desert rock were shipped from Barstow to Sacramento to create the Candlerock Lounge at Country Club Lanes in Sacramento. Expert stone mason Joe Mascarin poured the terrazzo and fitted together the stone for Covina Bowl in 1956 and stood by his work, grinding and polishing it to keep it fresh for decades. The same went for stained but unpainted boards used for ceilings, and natural cork repurposed as an acoustical material. Powers showed off an enormous forty-foot beam that supported the ceiling of Java Lanes to the reporter from *Bowlers Journal*. "We created a dramatic effect by designing this high ceiling," he told a reporter in 1959. "What would we have gained by covering the natural wood with plaster and paint? Nothing."

Water effects were in use at several centers, from fountains and ponds to a massive, cascading waterfall inside the multi-level dining room at Willow Grove Park Lanes. DeRosa fought to preserve existing trees and to keep an existing body of water on the site that dated back to its time as a Victorian-era amusement park. In his Waterfall Room, five hundred gallons of water continuously spilled over high stone shelves into a pool every sixty seconds, forming sheets as tall as the room. "We never keep it on for very long at a time," manager Stanley Raytinsky told a reporter in 1963. "Some people find it a little tiring." If one could avert their gaze from that spectacle,

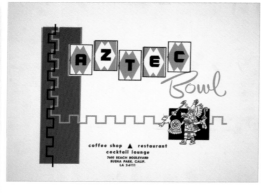

Top: Vivid and enticing menus from Azusa, Los Angeles, and Buena Park, California centers enhance the themes. ◆ Bottom: The golden lounge at Gil Hodges Lanes (1961, architect unknown) in Brooklyn was owned by the former Brooklyn Dodgers star and displayed baseball memorabilia inside.

the bar itself was finished in circles of multicolored luminescent Italian mosaic. The whole composition was bathed in a purple light.

At the other end of the design spectrum was the wide array of new plastics and synthetic materials developed around the war years. These were perhaps most visible in space age lighting fixtures, but plastics were an integral part of everything from roof shapes to indoor seating. The dynamic tension that comes from mixing the primitive and the modern is a key component of the style. In his book *Googie: Fifties Coffee Shop Architecture*, Alan Hess perfectly describes a googie coffee shop as a place where "Fred Flintstone and George Jetson could meet over a cup of coffee."

The DuPont Company was at the forefront of materials science by the 1950s, having already given the world Lucite and Teflon. Lee Heavy Wilton carpet in DuPont 501 continuous filament nylon was just the thing to stand up to twenty-four-hour-a-day exposure to heavy foot traffic, and food and

Brunswick produced a promotional film to introduce their Gold Crown Line in 1960. *The Golden Years* was preserved by the Library of Congress National Audio-Visual Conservation Center.

drink spills. Many months after installation at Parkway Bowl in El Cajon, the miracle fiber was still said to sparkle like new.

Plastic furnishings were easy to keep clean and looking bright and new. They were made in any color and, unlike the old wood benches, could never develop splinters or need refinishing. The Sjostrom company was among the small manufacturers turning out modernist furnishings for the lanes, promoting their "Jubilee" line in seven-layer, wear-resistant, polyester fiberglass. Brunswick may have made more fiberglass furniture than any other maker, with some of it still in service more than sixty years later. Brunswick utilized the same clean, modern lines in their line of billiards equipment, which found a home in many bowling centers.

The "Gold Crown" line became ubiquitous and everything from ball returns to seating to ashtrays were the pinnacle of space age design. This is the moment that Brunswick fully embraced modernism and there was no turning back. To launch the new light and sculpted new line, the Jam Handy Organization, a well-known industrial film production company in Detroit, was hired to create a fourteen-minute color promotional film in 1960 titled *The Golden Years*. This film, preserved by the Library of Congress, is a masterpiece of industrial filmmaking, incredible propaganda, and as much of a beautiful showcase for American industrial design and styling as classics such as *The American Look* or *Design For Dreaming* produced by General Motors. Brunswick had long sought to elevate bowling from the saloon, but now they were also trying to extricate it from the blue-collar beer drinkers in search of those well-off and clean cut suburban families filling the new cul-de-sacs. The film opens to a glorious swelling orchestral fanfare. Fade in to a soundstage where mom, dad, and their 2.3 nuclear children are in the dark, practicing

Families fill the lanes of a California bowling center in a scene captured for *Life* magazine in 1958. ◆ Opposite: The Candlerock coffee shop at Country Club Lanes (1960, Powers, Daly & DeRosa) in Sacramento was open twenty-four hours and offered plush surroundings and reasonable prices.

a challenge; Rossmor Lanes in Orange County solved this problem by adding a three-foot neutral buffer between the "authentic" peaked roof and beamed ceiling of the Old English steak house, and the rectilinear lines of the modern bowling center. Design that solves problems and makes life more efficient is one thing, but creating an environment that piques interest and brings people back might lead to crafting a successful imaginary world, whether it's modernism, nostalgia, or fantasy.

A good bar interior should hold your attention while you're sober and completely entrance you when you're not. You should be absolutely overwhelmed by the story unfolding around you, from the characters and symbols on the matchbook cover to the fully realized fine art crafted to transport you to Ancient Greece (at Arena Bowl), Rome (at Nave Lanes), or Egypt (at Covina Bowl and Sands Bowl in Lancaster).

A hedonistic night out could include an epicurean adventure, or at least the promise of visiting a faraway place. Essayist D.J. Waldie once described restaurants like these as "a simulation of something not quite real to begin with." A theme might begin and end with a clever name for your bar. There were plenty of German Hofbraus, and a few

Proprietor Stan Howard looks out from a trio of cards showcasing his venues within Wonder Bowl (1959, Daniel, Mann, Johnson and Mendenhall) in Downey. Top: The Jim Jeffries bar; Center: The Wonder Bowl coffee shop, home of the "Wonderburger"; Bottom: The "Hot Dawg" stand, where "No one over 21 is permitted."

Twin staircases frame a stone nook with a capiz shell lamp at Tropicana Lanes (1959, H.W. Underhill) and its Kon Tiki Room in Inglewood, California.

Large mixed media resin figures in the Masquerade Room at Beverly Bowling Center (1960, Chapman, McCorkel & Associates) in Montebello, California loom over bar patrons.

"Magic Carpet" theme was pure fiction, but Lagorio, inspired by her study of Sienese Quattrocento paintings, Byzantine mosaics, Etruscan frescoes, and her own vivid imagination, created a sparkling, color-soaked pleasure palace in the rich jewel tones and golden accents she saw in her head. The complex vision required all hands on deck to open on time. A crew of a dozen women were hired to hand-string 470,000 beads hung from the ceiling. Architect Austin Daly pitched in by staying up all night moving Lagorio's ladder around the room as she inscribed Arabic characters in gold leaf above the bar. Lagorio took the viewer on a journey to her own playful vision, whether in an original painting or in a psychedelic fantasy playing out in full color and three dimensions. She spoke about one work inspired by a friend's vibrant account of a recent desert trip and how she turned it into something otherworldly. "A letter I received while he was on this odyssey," she later wrote, "was so descriptive . . .

I became caught in the magic of it all."

Barbara Davis of West Covina was hired to create "unusual" murals and "unique" decorations for the Pyramid Room at Covina Bowl, the first of the elaborately themed lounges. Davis studied at Chouinard Art Institute and ArtCenter in Los Angeles, and was a decorator for stores and residences, as well as the Officers Club at the China Lake Naval Base and the Hotel Matador in Palm Springs. Davis crafted custom lighting fixtures for the showroom, but her major work in the lounge was an eighty-foot-long mixed-media work combining bronze and oils with copper and wire sculpture. Davis spent a great deal of time studying photographs of the tomb of Thebes and her work depicted Cleopatra and queens of the Fourth Egyptian Dynasty. Ancient alien enthusiasts may wonder why the modernist steel fireplace in the Pyramid Room had tiny holes pierced through the hood, that flames could be seen through, depicting Capricorn, Polaris, and

Mosaic artist Murray Large created this study for an epic mosaic artwork at El Dorado Lanes (1959, Ron Cleveland) in the Westchester neighborhood of Los Angeles, California.

constellations. Themes can be complicated! Two years later and an hour north, the creators of the Sands Bowl in Lancaster also adopted the trappings of ancient Egypt inside its Nile Room, covering a 180-degree rotunda with polychrome art depicting a banquet in a wraparound mural that filled the room. Artist Milton Tuttle of Culver City and his partner Olin Sherrod chose to render twenty-two life-sized Egyptian characters in an unusual Sgraffito art technique, which, if not as old as the pharaohs, at least reached back to the Italian Renaissance. Tuttle and Sherrod, who helped revive the art form, claimed to be the first modern American practitioners. One-quarter-inch layers of Portland cement plaster tinted in different colors with dry pigment are carefully laid over each other in a specific consistency. By reverse carving designs into the wet cement, different colors on successive layers are exposed.

Tuttle was a commercial artist who trained at the Bisttram School of Fine Arts in Los Angeles and worked in Las Vegas, Denver, Palm Springs, and all over Southern California. He met the artist Rex Horn in Holland after his World War II service and learned the ancient technique. Early artists were limited to two colors, but Tuttle and Sherrod were able to coax seven shades from the plaster. The pair were helped by master plasterer Howard Porter and another artist, Florence Ferman, who studied at UCLA and exhibited her works at the Pasadena Art Museum and LACMA. "It's an extremely delicate process," her developer husband, Jack, pointed out at the time. "The plaster layers must be put on one right after the other, and then the carving must begin while the plaster is still damp. Once the work has started, the artists can't quit until the rendering is complete. Sometimes this involves working well into the night with the aid of floodlights." The Fermans were world travelers who used their collection of color slides to study the art of

ancient civilizations. "We pick an historical era such as ancient Greece, Egypt, or Babylon that seems to fit the particular building and community," Ferman said. "And then reproduce some of that era's most famous works in Sgraffito."

Tuttle loved the unique, dimensional quality and durability of Sgraffito and would go on to create monumental artworks indoors and out. A twenty-six-foot-high replica of a wooden mask from Tami Island in Huon Gulf, New Guinea, survives at the "Polynesia" apartment building in Canoga Park; scantily clad islanders at the Glenlani Tiki apartments in West Los Angeles; and a monumental pre-Columbian work fronting the Barkley building at Laurel Canyon and Weddington Avenues in North Hollywood. Another surviving Tuttle, an abstract modernist work on the Executive Towers (1963, Al Beadle) in Phoenix is prominent on a complex listed on the National Register of Historic Places. "Murals will chip in time, and mosaic work may lose bits and pieces here and there," Tuttle said in 1963. "But Sgraffito is forever."

Milton Tuttle became a proponent for sgraffito art in the 1950s and used it throughout his projects. This 1957 work from a private collection evokes his lost Egyptian figures at Sands Bowl (1958) in Lancaster, California.

CHAPTER 5

ENTERTAINMENT

Organist Gil Rosas at the keys in the Mural Room of the Fiesta Bowl (1958, William Rudolph) in Santa Barbara, California, soon after it opened in 1958.

WHEN **NEW BOWLING CENTER** pleasure palaces opened, they were like whole cities that just floated down from space. Every new site, from the tiniest eight-laner to the lavish luxury complexes that sprawled across more than one hundred lanes (looking at you, Willow Grove) had a bar, the one tradition that was carried over from the saloon days of the nineteenth century. Many were simple counters where players could fill their beer glasses and take it straight to the lanes; others had a call button on a space age console that would summon a cocktail waitress who would bring players drinks. (Some

proprietors reported that nearly 80% of liquor sales were on the lanes.) The special centers, the biggies, could always be counted on for a second bar (and sometimes more), a coffee shop, and often a fine dining restaurant among the amenities.

A 1972 United States Department of Commerce study of bowling centers noted that sales of food and drink were an operator's second biggest revenue source. The larger the center, the greater the percentage of dining to total income. The Feds found that an establishment earning $65,000 a year generated 80% of its income from bowling, while one earning $475,000 took in 40 to 50% of its revenue from bowling fees. Different types of liquor licenses played a part in how much space was devoted to dining, with some jurisdictions requiring a full kitchen and some satisfied with a vending machine for sandwiches.

Decorative themes transported diners away from their humdrum life to a different universe, even if only for the time it took to finish a cocktail, and they were an integral part of the entertainment environment in Southern California. The theming trend began at the Panama-Pacific Exposition in San

Top: A tiki guards the entrance to Kona Kove at Stardust Bowl (1960, Armet & Davis) in West Covina, California. ◆ Bottom: The dynamic entrance to the Candlerock Lounge at Country Club Lanes (1960, Powers, Daly & DeRosa) in Sacramento, California. ◆ Opposite: SEAGRAMS advertised itself as "America's Bowling Nightcap"; this advertisement from 1961 depicted a group of upscale young bowlers on the lanes with their own bartender pouring Seagrams 7 Crown.

Left: A packed house celebrates the new year at showbiz impresario Paul Catalana's Safari Room inside Plaza Lanes (1960, architect unknown) in San Jose, California. ◆ Right: Organ player in the Golden Circle Room at Yosemite Lanes (1961, Paul Wong) in Modesto, California.

Diego in 1915, which whisked visitors around ancient Mexico and MesoAmerica. In Los Angeles, restaurants like the Tam O'Shanter, designed by Hollywood set designer Harry Oliver, offered a wee dram of Scotch in a fantasy environment reminiscent of a cottage in the Scottish highlands. Every location of Los Angeles's legendary Clifton's Cafeteria told a story from fantasy islands to dark forests that dispatched diners to distant enchanting worlds far from the hardscrabble life that might cause them to take advantage of the restaurant's credo, established during the Great Depression, that "no one will be turned away for lack of funds."

The years following World War II saw an unprecedented economic boom that created a large middle class. The vast resources marshaled into production for war equipment were once again available to make refrigerators and washing machines. Meat and sugar were rationed, and then all of a sudden they weren't, and after a decade of economic depression and years of war restrictions, folks could suddenly catch up. Some went much further than that, reinventing themselves with a new home, a new car, a new family, and a whole new life in what had previously been an orange grove or a dairy farm.

The suddenly prosperous, suddenly married, suddenly suburban families of 1950s America enjoyed the American dream with no-money-down loans available to returning servicemen, and, in a country with mandatory military service, there were millions of returning G.I.s. For all the social strife in mid-century America, '50s suburbia offered such favorable economics that a family could thrive on a single income.

After parking the tail-finned, two-tone family cruiser in the garage, outfitting a sparkling new home with an indoor barbecue and remote-control television, and filling those high interest savings accounts with the leftovers, what to do with the rest of this overflowing pot of moolah? Go to Vegas!

As the hotels on the Las Vegas strip grew in size, they grew in flashiness, attempting to outdo one another. Each one of them featured a big showroom, and these nightclubs attracted the most famous singers, dancers, and comedians in the country. Many of them added a second, smaller venue for overflow. The new lounges often booked lesser-known acts, but through the 1950s they developed a zeitgeist of their own. Headline acts would often drop in on the lounge before or after their own shows. The performers shared a camaraderie. "Frank Sinatra used to say that after they did their shows in Vegas, they'd go watch Buddy Greco in the lounge," Welsh singer Tom Jones told PBS's Charlie Rose. Covina Bowl architect Gordon Powers is one of the direct connections between the lounges in Las Vegas and the California bowling showrooms. "I did a lot of work for Moe Dalitz in Vegas," Powers remembered. "He treated me like his son.

He was a bootlegger from Cleveland, he went out to Vegas and built the Desert Inn."

When Powers was pitching the Brutocao brothers on the wonders he had in mind for Covina Bowl, he suggested they add a Las Vegas-style lounge and call it the Pyramid Room. "We made kind of a study and we said you've got to have a bar anyway, so put in a nightclub," Powers said. "They spent over $360,000 of their own money and they made it all back the first year."

Henry and Dorris Levant, who owned farmland not too far from the movie studios of the San Fernando Valley, hired Powers, Daly & DeRosa to develop their property into the Reseda Bowl. "A number of developers came by to

Cocktail napkins are the most delicate survivors. A trio saved from Covina Bowl (1956, Powers, Daly & DeRosa), Lucky Lanes (1960, Goodwin Steinberg), and Camino Bowl (1959, Powers, Daly & DeRosa).

purchase our land to build a bowling alley," their son Glenn remembers. "My father said, 'well, it couldn't be that hard,' so he built one. He didn't know a thing about it." The novice investors were hesitant to invest in a lavish lounge. "I don't think we had the seating capacity to make big name shows economically feasible," says Glen.

The lounges became a hub for cultural happenings and a new town square for the bedroom communities. Comedian John Barbour remembered, "When they came to the bowling alley showroom they were dressed up. They weren't going to get dressed up for bowling; they were dressed for a show. Men wore suits, women wore gowns and you got a Vegas show." When the Brutocao brothers again approached Powers's firm to design their new Anaheim Bowl, the theme was upgraded from ancient Egypt to imperial Rome. The Chariot Room advertised itself as "Where Las Vegas entertainment and Anaheim meet."

The gourmet restaurant was a hallmark of the most lavish new bowling centers, whether these rooms advertised a celebrity chef, innovations like a charcoal broiler, or an entire display case filled with their finest meats, allowing the diner to select their own steak. For decades, steak and lobster were hallmarks on the French-inspired menus of the finest of big city fine dining establishments. The rich dishes brought the elegance and sophistication bowling proprietors craved at their upscale restaurant, and found their way to menus at

their establishments. Soft lighting, white tablecloths, and sumptuous leather booths lent the same air of sophistication you might find at the Brown Derby to your neighborhood bowling alley.

In the agricultural hub of Salinas, California, a new restaurant opened with the Valley Center Bowl in 1957. The dining room accommodated 125 people in a cherry-paneled room,

All the elements of a classic tiki bar line up at Kona Kove in the Stardust Bowl (1960, Armet & Davis) in West Covina, California.

with red and black carpeting and chartreuse ceilings. It was helmed by chef Andre Martini, who started his cooking career catering private Hollywood parties at the homes of Louis B. Mayer and William Randolph Hearst, and feeding entire film sets like the full cast and crew of *Gone with the Wind* at MGM Studios. Martini relocated to Northern California after a long stint at the celebrity-studded Chianti restaurant in Hollywood. He brought his recipes for continental cuisine to Monterey County. Prime rib and boneless squab were served in his Copper Room until 10 p.m. every night.

Another MGM chef, Thomas Burke, ended up in charge of all dining facilities at Corbin Bowl in Tarzana. He had spent the previous three decades as *chef de cuisine* at the Mocambo nightclub, Preston Sturges's Players Club on the Sunset Strip, and the Ambassador and Biltmore Hotels in Los Angeles. Italian chef Louis Paini of Nave Lanes in Novato had a resume that included Los Angeles's most famous restaurants: Chasen's, Romanoff's, and the Brown Derby. One can only assume he considered his new gig an upgrade.

Famous chefs in Los Angeles often ended

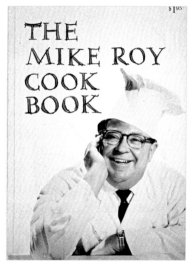

Celebrity chef Mike Roy was a longtime TV and radio star who took over restaurants at Hollywood Legion Lanes (1959, William L. Rudolph) in Hollywood and Orange Bowl (1957, Underhill & Wagner) in Rialto, California.

up on television, and folksy Mike Roy enjoyed promoting his endless stream of cookbooks. Roy was food editor on KNX radio with commentaries about Los Angeles's best food and drink, and was a CBS radio personality for years. In 1946, a year before James Beard went on TV in New York, Roy created *Secrets of a Gourmet*—what could be America's first televised cooking show—on experimental station W6XAO (later CBS Channel 2, the first station in Los Angeles). He added wine commentary on a new show for KTLA called *Mike Roy's Kitchen* in 1950. "I don't know much about wine, but I do know what the people like," he told a wine judge at the Los Angeles County Fair. "Mine is a people's palate."

What a coup for the Orange Bowl in Rialto, an hour outside of Los Angeles, when it announced that Roy was their *maître d'* and new head chef when the Bowling Green restaurant opened there in 1957. Roy had been a showman since he was a teenager in North Dakota announcing basketball games on air. He was an announcer for TV pioneer Dave Garroway, the first host of NBC's *Today* show, and emceed the Charlie McCarthy and Abbott and Costello shows. The populist favorite created

Left: The Del Rays lit up the stage at West Lane Bowl (1960, Rudolph and Associates) in Stockton, California, in 1963. ◆ Right: An elegant audience dressed up for a night on the town having fun at the Safari Room at Plaza Lanes (1960, architect unknown) in San Jose, California.

"a sumptuous menu of the finest foods," noted a review at the time, "at moderate prices." Three years later, he took over the menu at Hollywood Legion Lanes where he helped create their "Stadium Room" restaurant, which offered both a "Steak Buffet" and a "Las Vegas Style Breakfast" that ran all night, starting at 10 p.m.

A full range of tropical cocktails served in coconuts joined abalone and frog legs meuniere on the menu, along with top-notch entertainment, at the Safari Room in San Jose's Plaza Lanes. Down the road at Saratoga Lanes's Brave Bull restaurant, rack of

lamb and New York steak were served on oak planks. Their massive, wood-grained menu also featured South African lobster tail and a Caesar salad prepared tableside. For dessert, you could order cherries jubilee or baked Alaska, which was served on fire! The after-dinner drink menu was even more sumptuous with ice cream Grasshoppers and cocktails made with exotic liqueurs like Tuaca, Strega, and Fior d'Alpi. All this in a bowling alley some fifty miles from the posh hotel bars of big city San Francisco. The Friar Room at Serra Bowl offered an elegant Mother's Day brunch, and venues like Santa Ana's Hunt Club that wanted to attract mom, dad, and the kids to have a posh dinner together might institute a "Family Club." Walt Disney loved old-fashioned soda fountains and the center played to their youthful clientele with the "King Pin," "Strike," and "Spare" sundaes and "flaming sodas" at the pink-and-white ice cream parlor at Celebrity Sports Center in Denver.

Workers at the nearby Lincoln-Mercury plant were among the patrons of Mercury Bowl and its restaurant in Pico Rivera, but owner Dave Boran sat at a table rattling off only the highest powered visitors when

An authentic mid-century color palette with a star-filled ceiling shines at the Pyramid Room at Covina Bowl (1956, Powers, Daly & DeRosa) in Covina, California. Egyptian reliefs by artist Barbara Davis.

Bowlers Journal dropped the establishment it described as "dolled up in a sky blue, space age motif" with "satellite chandeliers and celestial ceilings" in 1959. "Stanley Mosk sat in that chair the other day," he said. "He is Attorney General of California." He went on to mention congressmen, media moguls, judges, mayors, sheriffs, and some of the most powerful men in the state as patrons of his center.

The fine dining restaurants and showrooms may have been less popular with the leagues and the day players, who often wanted to spend most of their time on the lanes, but they drew a clientele from the neighbors in the new upscale neighborhoods, which were as new as the bowling center itself. These same suburbanites filled the restaurants, finding fine dining in a new community that may not have had many options. The first line of strip development often included hamburger stands and car-oriented quick-service restaurants. Fine dining establishments were fewer and more profound. The costumed *maître d'*, live music, white tablecloth restaurants, and all the amenities that the new suburbanites remembered from the big city were finally coming to their tract. In a bowling center, miles from town. Who are we to understand the customs of this long-gone civilization?

The luxury didn't last and many of the seriously luxe establishments were short-lived. The menus pivoted, outside operators took over the spaces, and sometimes they cycled through multiple identities before settling

into a long, slow decline. By the time Covina Bowl's Pyramid Room closed, it was a stripped-down banquet hall. The most deluxe features were slowly eroded from the centers the way wind and sand have smoothed the Sphinx. Over time, the table lanterns disappeared and the white tablecloths stopped being set. The chefs became less pedigreed and simplified and streamlined the menu, losing difficult dishes as the venues stopped ordering matchbooks, and their unique name and themes were forgotten. Slapdash repairs, broken signs, decluttering, and "modernizing" of the spaces made them into wide open venues for rock concerts or cheap rentals.

One of the best remaining original lounges, the former Red Coach Room at La Habra "300" Bowl in Orange County, California, was once an old English-themed lounge with plush banquettes, wood paneling, and stained glass. After a violent altercation following a punk show in 2015, they lost their live entertainment license and switched to karaoke. The original illuminated sign featuring the antique carriage advertising the wood-paneled lounge drifted away over time, and was more recently painted with lettering over the woodwork

Top: Java Lanes builder Henry Cox (right) with manager Dick Fletcher and their wives enjoy an evening at the East Indies room in Java Lanes (1958, Powers, Daly & DeRosa) in Long Beach, California. ◆ Bottom: Themed menu from the East Indies room at Java Lanes (1958, Powers, Daly & DeRosa) in Long Beach, California.

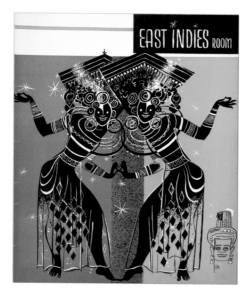

that reads "13th Frame Lounge."

How would anyone rocking out in the worn-out and stripped-down "Lava Lounge" at the Long Beach, California, Java Lanes, where '90s stars like Weezer and Lit got their start, know it had once been a glamorous nightspot known as the "East Indies Room," tract home developer Henry Cox as an homage to the Pacific Island culture he was so enamored with? Cox also built the tiki-themed Kona Lanes in Costa Mesa, some twenty miles down the coast from Java Lanes, not far from the docks where he moored his teak and mahogany yacht *Coral Seas*, whose name was gold-leafed in the same sort of Chinese brush stroke lettering on his custom bowling shirt and on the massive Las Vegas-style neon sign at Kona Lanes. Cox hired a studio artist to paint a giant mural of a Polynesian scene in his home dining room.

Something of a lounge circuit emerged, with acts traveling between showrooms in Las Vegas, Reno, Lake Tahoe, and the bowling lounges of California. Outside of the largest venues, like the Safari Room at Plaza Lanes in San Jose, the acts were typically lesser known, but still sang and danced their hearts out for appreciative audiences who had left big city luxuries behind when they inhabited the hinterlands.

Kitty Kover was a singer and dancer who had starred in the "Casino de Paris" show at the Dunes Hotel, and at Dean Martin's Dino's Lodge on Hollywood's Sunset Strip. One reviewer described the scantily clad performer as a "shapely lass who doesn't mind showing off her shapely gams." She was signed to Brunswick Records, a record label which started as a division of the bowling equipment manufacturer. When Kover was booked at the Stardust Room at Comet Lanes in Chatsworth, a reporter noted that she earned more than she did at the more well-known nightclubs. Duke Ellington, Cab Calloway, and Bing Crosby all recorded under the Brunswick label before it was bought by CBS.

The Salmas Brothers, longtime favorites

The majority of bowling lounge performers traveled a circuit of restaurants and nightclubs in Los Angeles and Las Vegas. Singer and dancer Kitty Kover (left) once starred opposite Jayne Mansfield in a production of *Gentlemen Prefer Blondes*. The Salmas Brothers (right) billed themselves as "The Fabulous Greeks"; audience members compared lead singer Guy Salmas to Dean Martin.

Original entrance sign from the Jester Room lounge at Kingpin Lanes (1961, Arthur Froehlich) in Los Angeles, California.

in Las Vegas, were the opening act at the Chariot Room. The five Greek siblings from Detroit were represented by Joe Rollo, a talent agent in Beverly Hills. "He had a reputation as a thief," comedian Jackie Curtiss told historian Kliph Nesteroff. "Joe Rollo Agency made a contract out for twenty-five hundred dollars and then tells you you're only getting fifteen. So he got a thousand dollars plus ten percent of our fifteen hundred. We found out later this was called double contracting."

The Brutocaos at Covina Bowl booked practically the entire cast of *The Lawrence Welk Show* with Rocky Rockwell, "Champagne Lady" Roberta Linn, and "Big" Tiny Little, with each playing three shows a night, starting the last one at midnight. Welk's entire orchestra entertained the bowling writers banquet at his Hollywood Palladium in 1961. Showbiz deals took place in the lounges, like the time Willie Ito of *The Jetsons* offered Scatman Crothers the voice of Hong Kong Phooey after seeing him perform at Hollywood Legion Lanes.

New Year's Eve was always an occasion to showcase the biggest name acts. In 1963, the Brutocaos hired future *Laugh-In* hosts Dan Rowan and Dick Martin to emcee, a

year earlier they had featured jazz singer Mel Tormé, and the brothers booked movie bombshell Mamie Van Doren for a December 31st show at their Anaheim Bowl.

Grammy winner Louis Armstrong, one of the most influential jazz artists in history, played a stint at the Roaring '20s room at Parkway Bowl in San Diego. Another Louis from New Orleans, Louis Prima, was reportedly the highest paid entertainer in Las Vegas when he played the same room.

The names on the marquee at the Safari Room, located in Plaza Lanes in San Jose, shined as bright as the ones on the Las Vegas strip: Lionel Hampton, Della Reese, Nancy Wilson, and The Supremes. All that and a second bar called The Monkey Room with Slim Gaillard doing music and comedy ad libs at the piano. The kings of Exotica, Martin Denny and Arthur Lyman, both performed in the room, as did the cornerstones of the Las Vegas lounge, Buddy Greco and the Mary Kaye Trio.

The club's owner was Paul Catalana, who first brought the Beatles to San Francisco in 1964 and bought his first movie theater at twenty-five. By the mid-1960s, the showman owned three drive-ins, six apartment houses, two dozen fancy watches, and a trio of miniature blue poodles. "The whole picture's changed," Catalana told the *San Francisco Examiner*. "People like to go out of town now for their entertainment. I bring in national stars."

Not all stars were sold on the power of the lounge. Edgy comedian John Barbour came to the Chariot Room with hesitation. "I was reluctant because bowling alleys to me meant lower classes, but when I went there it was like a Las Vegas showroom," he remembered. "The audience was dressed up for a show. Men wore suits and women wore gowns. If you go to Vegas now they look like they came from Wal-Mart." Barbour played the Brutocao clubs through the mid-1960s. "Anaheim Bowl was by far the most glamorous," he says today. "It was the Caesars Palace of bowling alleys."

John Buzon, an organ player from Pittsburgh, reinvented his band in Los Angeles. "We had been playing with a society-type group and the leader walked off one Sunday night," Buzon told the *Reno Gazette-Journal* in 1963. "It looked like the end of our musical careers. We had nothing to lose so we decided to swing on our last night." A talent scout from Liberty Records was in the audience and their first album with Liberty, *Inferno*, came out a few months later, followed by *Cha Cha on the Rock*s. "Neither the boys individually or as a group consider themselves jazz musicians," the liner notes on *Inferno* proclaim. "But rather swing musicians with a drive. They generate some really great and enthusiastic jazz both on the torchy ballads and the sizzling swingers." Buzon played much larger lounges in Lake Tahoe and Reno, and even opened for Louis Prima and Keely Smith with Sam Butera, but "he talked about Covina Bowl all the time," his daughter Karen remembered. "I don't think it's ideally what

Left: Diana Ross and the Supremes perform at the Safari Room at Plaza Lanes (1960, architect unknown) in San Jose, California. ◆ Right: Jazz trio performing at the Pacific Bowl (1960, architect unknown) in Oakland, California, during the 1960s.

Top: Jazz legend Mel Tormé and B-movie queen Mamie Van Doren headlined New Year's Eve shows at LA-area bowling centers in 1962. ◆ Bottom: *Knockers Up!* was one of the many hit records from bawdy singer Rusty Warren. The comedy queen recorded several live albums at Anaheim Bowl. The title is a pun on the wooden table knockers audiences would clack while applauding.

old are you? Have you ever seen Rusty Warren?" Gordon Powers chuckled at an interview in the Covina Bowl in 2014. "It's all risqué, double entendre stuff and she packed 'em in!" The flashy redhead made her name at Covina and Anaheim Bowls before headlining Las Vegas, New York's Copacabana and Latin Quarter, and Gene Norman's Crescendo on Hollywood's Sunset Strip. She hit it big with more than a dozen party records including *Knockers Up!, Songs For Sinners*, and *Rusty Warren Bounces Back*. The *New York Times* described her as a "brash comic in a strait-laced time" whose comedy resonated with "women who were getting ready to shed the straitjackets of the day." Warren graduated from the New England Conservatory of Music, and was conducted by Arthur Fiedler at Boston's Tanglewood Music Festival, but it was through her sexy humor that she finally found her audience.

"Rusty broke

he wanted to do, but I think he had a pretty cool thing going there. He certainly had a following and recorded several albums."

One of the most prolific acts ever to play the bowling circuit, Rusty Warren, made her name with "blue" comedy albums recorded live in the lounge. "How

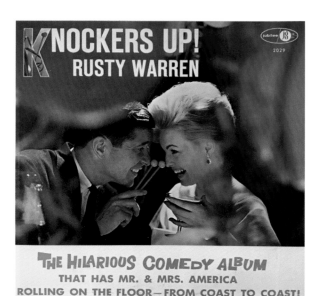

THE POPULARIZATION OF BOWLING in the suburbs followed the mass exodus out of the big cities after World War II, and the subsequent decline of urban centers. Streetcar lines declined as more emphasis was put on automobile traffic after President Eisenhower signed the Federal-Aid Highway Act in 1956. Downtown entertainments suffered; many of the cavernous movie palaces fell into disuse and disrepair. Some operators turned to bowling as one possible salvation, converting their auditoriums into bowling lanes. Movie stars, sports stars, and the greats of bowling were sought out to endorse and invest in ever more lavish entertainment centers—whether they had an interest in the game or not.

With thousands of new lanes opening, efforts were made to expand the audience for bowling and welcome newcomers to the game. Bowling facilities became recreation centers, with boosters creating new language modified to reflect the suburban feel. Alleys became lanes and gutters became channels. And not all of this was hyperbole. Pickwick Bowl in Burbank was a full-fledged recreation center with swimming pools, billiard rooms, a riding stable, two restaurants, and a ballroom.

The new centers were often open twenty-four hours, and frequently provided the only gathering places in a new town. There was a natural isolation in the boondocks, which may have been orange groves just a few months earlier. Bowling centers took their place alongside cul-de-sacs and backyard barbecues as icons of suburbia. Formal and casual meetings took place in these new banquet rooms, from political rallies and service club meetings to life milestones like birthdays and weddings. Bowling became a substitute for the walkable urban core; the place where suburbanites could find community and where people with little in common could mix.

"The bowling center may well be the one social center which draws people of all faiths together in many suburban communities," architect Richard Barancik told *Bowlers Journal* in 1961.

Much community social life is based on religious group activities. In new suburbs there is no real main street

Developer R.H. Farrell and Miss Sylmar, Mary Ann Davis, hold a rendering of the proposed 1962 Ronnell Bowl in Sylmar, California, as business manager C.J. Evron and architect William Rudolph look on, October, 1961.

or meeting center. The new suburbanites, [depend] on their autos to get around and they're not always able to find any real community life. The nearly universal interest in bowling may be the one thing that brings together new neighbors, not only of different religious backgrounds, but from every occupation, financial status, and age. It can turn out to be the starting point of a solid community life that distinguishes a real community from a collection of houses.

Women, children, seniors, teenagers, and entire family groups were encouraged to join

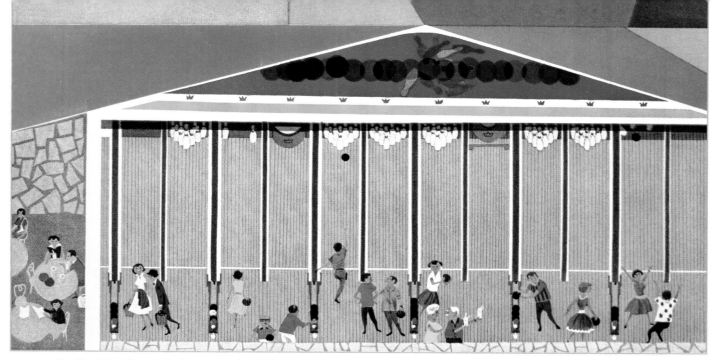

Top: Detail from Brunswick advertisement highlighting the company's varied divisions, from school furnishings to hospital equipment to entire bowling centers. ◆ Bottom: KWOW 1600 was a tiny country-and-western station in the San Gabriel Valley that set up a DJ booth inside Covina Bowl (1956, Powers, Daly & DeRosa) for their *Ten Pin Alley* show.

in the fun, with special programs and services tailored to each group. As the atmosphere of the centers rose in sophistication and comfort, additional amenities were added, and newcomers came to expect them as standard. Of course, new centers would have free parking and the latest equipment. But did you hear about the one down the road with the great lounge acts? Or the one with the uniformed nurses caring for children at no charge?

"There were no day care centers except in bowling centers," says proprietor Rick Golobic. "It's where mom could get a morning off." Kiddie rooms were no stranger to excess. Air conditioning was commonplace there when it was still rare in homes and cars. Electronic controls adjusted lights, and intercoms

allowed immediate communication from the lanes. The most advanced centers offered closed-circuit TV so moms could keep one eye on the lane and the other on the nursery. "Everything was child-size, down to the toilets," says Nancy Castro, whose father built Java Lanes in 1958. Five thousand youngsters cycled through the nursery at Hart Bowl in Dallas during one sixty-day period in 1960. "The children have their noses wiped and are placed under the nursery attendant's supervision," reported *Today's*

Top: Supervised children's nurseries made it possible for women to enjoy bowling, too. Eva Johnson, assistant nursery attendant at Covina Bowl, keeps kids happy with a cracker snack in 1957. ◆ Bottom: Moms and their children at Paramus Lanes (1955, architect unknown) in Paramus, New Jersey.

Health, a journal of the American Medical Association in 1961.

Willow Grove Park Lanes offered kids use of toy trains, ships, a life-sized rocking horse, and a play sculpture described as a "half-sized Moby Dick." Some playrooms were finished with cork and heavy carpet to keep the noise level down. "People got excited! Here was something new where mom and dad could take the kids," says Golobic. "Here's a place where women could go drink a Ramos Fizz at 9 o'clock in the morning. You could have three little kids and stick 'em in this room with this nice lady and thousands of dollars of toys and it didn't cost you anything. It was an incredible respite." As one old timer put it at the time, "I bowled for twenty-eight years before I ever saw a woman in a bowling center." By 1961, bowling was the biggest competitive sport for women in America. Eight million women spent almost $1.2 billion annually on bowling.

As soon as kids could hold a bowling ball, they were out of the nursery and onto the lanes. "I was too small even to wear bowling shoes," Von Mueller's son Gil says. "I bowled in my socks. They gave me a six-pound ball, and I used two hands to throw it." Craig Schene of Fon-Ri Lanes in Rialto remembered, "My mom bowled on a league. My dad bowled on a league. My older sister was on a league. I was on a league. We were all on separate leagues."

Saturdays were often dedicated to children's leagues. Generally, the youngest bowlers were called PeeWees, Bantams were six-to-ten-year-olds, and Juniors were twelve-to-fifteen-year-olds. Older teens and collegiate teams had their own leagues. In 1961, the Del Rosa bowl in San Bernardino, California, had the largest junior bowling programs in the county with six hundred children attending every week. High schools and colleges started adding bowling lanes to campuses; some set up temporary arrangements in gymnasiums and other classes took place in bowling centers. Instead of a cash prize, the schools in Alhambra, California, awarded Hershey bars.

The offerings at Anaheim Bowl included special attractions for the kids like a

Left: Three-year-old Kevin West is a candidate for his family's team in Tallahassee, Florida in 1963. ◆ Right: The members of the first championship team in the Darby Township, Pennsylvania Junior bowling league beam proudly show their trophies in 1967. From left, back row: Stanley Bobo, and John Dandridge; Front row Duane McKnight, Tyrone Young, Otis Smith, and Drucilla Smith.

Flippy was not the only bowling dolphin. Lucky wowed audiences with his tenpin skills at Aquarama in Philadelphia in the 1960s.

merry-go-round, a ski slide, hobby horse, swings, and a pint-sized Ferris Wheel. Brunswick sent kid-friendly TV stars like Bozo the Clown to many grand openings, including at Garey Center Bowl in Pomona, California. And clowns weren't the only circus acts luring families. In 1962, a Brunswick Ambassador helped teach a dolphin to bowl. His trainer would throw a wooden ball into the water and "Flippy would dive after it, grab the ball in his powerful jaw, burst from the water, and with an underhead jerk of the head, flip it toward the land," *Bowlers Journal* reported. "Flippy averaged seven pins a throw."

But even Flippy couldn't attract as many kids as Chief Halftown, an entertainer and television star whose children's variety show

first aired in 1950. In 1958, he started a junior bowling tournament with televised finals attracting eight thousand youngsters from eight to sixteen, which ran for more than thirty-two years. He had been a pinboy as a child and was an avid bowler during World War II. Halftown was a full-blooded Seneca tribesman and direct descendant of the chief who signed the Seneca peace treaty with the US in 1794. Chief Halftown would show up at a bowling alley in traditional attire to entertain children, but he quickly realized that the kids would have more fun if he taught them to bowl. Instead of a simple meet-and-greet, he demonstrated the game and helped kids become better bowlers. He visited more than 250 cities in seven countries in Europe

kept her job as a court reporter to help pay travel expenses when Don booked an out-of-town tournament. "In the '60s, the first prize was $20,000, second was $10,000, and the lowest spot would be $2,000. You had to have a certain score to cash. But it wasn't all about the money. Don loved the game and was very charismatic. And the fans loved him." Scott signed autographs and posed for pictures after the games. "People want to talk to him. This is a celebrity. This is somebody of importance."

Don Scott wasn't the only celebrity who decided buying a bowling alley was a great way to invest his money. Baseball great Mickey Mantle was recruited by Brunswick and opened his own center in

Top: Pro bowler Don Scott on the lanes in the 1950s. Tire mogul Harvey Firestone Jr. asked Scott to help him reach Black audiences. ◆
Bottom: Ernie Moore teaches a group of girls to bowl at Pacific Bowl (1960, architect unknown) in Oakland, California, during the 1960s.

Dallas. Brunswick also helped major league football and baseball players who wanted to open their own centers once their sports career had come to an end. New York Yankees Mickey Mantle and Yogi Berra, heavyweight boxer Joe Lewis, and Baltimore Colts quarterback Johnny Unitas all opened namesake centers. Major league baseball star Irv Noren worked shifts behind the counter at Friendly Hills Lanes in Whittier, California, before opening his own center in Pasadena, California.

Comedian Harold Lloyd owned Llo-Da-Mar Bowl (1941, William Douglas Lee) in Santa Monica, California, but competed all over the world. He promoted the game for decades.

It wasn't just sports stars that wanted in on the action. Like Harold Lloyd, many producers and actors decided to try their hands at sponsoring teams and building their own centers. After all, there was an Inter-Studio League, and most studios sent players, including 20th Century Fox, MGM, Columbia, and Paramount. In 1961, it was estimated that as many as 25% of the establishments in Southern California had movie industry backing. Most stars were quiet investors; business folk from Aaron Spelling to Elmer Bernstein capitalized on the popularity of bowling. It was a passive investment for most, including actress Barbara Eden, who,

before she starred in *I Dream of Jeannie*, was part owner of Bowling Square in Arcadia with her husband, actor Michael Ansara. Eden's uncle Grandvell Shumaker was the developer behind the project, and while Eden became a better bowler after spending time there, the financing was more of a requital for a relative who supported the aspiring starlet when she arrived in Hollywood. "I didn't have anything to do with the business," she said recently. "They would have business meetings and I would be out on the lanes." Stars could leverage their fame to bring attention to a new endeavor. "We had a huge opening party and a lot of my actor friends came."

The pinnacles of red-blooded Americana wanted in on the game. Singing cowboy Roy Rogers invested in Reseda Lanes in Los Angeles's San Fernando Valley. But it took no less than Walt Disney to join up with other big star investors for the Celebrity Lanes (later known as Celebrity Sports Center) project near Denver. The mogul recruited Jack Benny, Spike Jones, Bing Crosby, and Charles Laughton as investors in the epic project, which included slot car races and a swimming pool so large that it could accommodate sailboat races. The mega-project on seven acres was budgeted at more than $6 million and opened in 1960.

TV was always part of the plans for the center, which was built with all the equipment necessary to broadcast across the country. Disney said, "There is a great need on the adult, teenage, and youth level for recreation. I have traveled to many parts of the world and have seen this need magnified. We believe we have here an answer." Benny was less introspective, "I know as much about bowling as Zsa Zsa Gabor does about housekeeping but I know it will make money."

Bowling touched every corner of American culture during its 1960s heyday, playing a part in evolving gender and family roles, sport and celebrity, art and architecture, and even race and politics. The White House installed a bowling alley in 1947, and a photo op on the lanes became a way for almost every president from Truman forward to connect with everyday Americans. The largest participation sport in America is for everybody.

Before she became a TV legend on *I Dream of Jeannie*, Barbara Eden was a successful actress who invested in her uncle's Bowling Square (1961, Jacobson & Coppedge) in Arcadia, California. "I used to have my bowling ball in a little bag but I think it was given to the Goodwill," she said in 2023. "Maybe I'll go back to it now."

CHAPTER 6

FALL AND RISE

The Bronco Bowl (1961, architect unknown) in Dallas, Texas once featured indoor archery, slot car racing, mini golf, and a concert hall, in addition to bowling lanes. It was a well-known music venue in the 1990s, hosting acts from Bob Dylan to Bruce Springsteen. It was demolished in 2003 and replaced by a Home Depot.

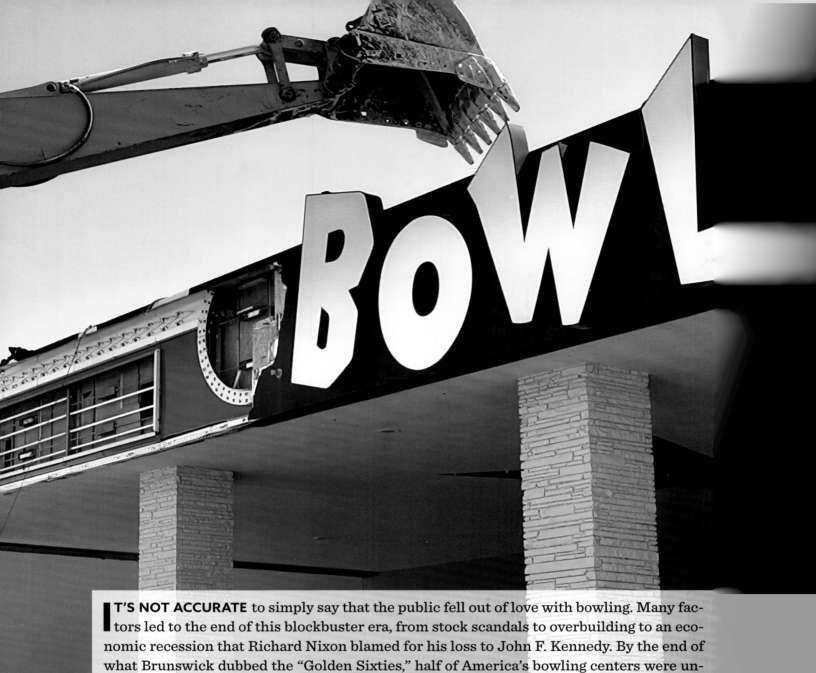

IT'S NOT ACCURATE to simply say that the public fell out of love with bowling. Many factors led to the end of this blockbuster era, from stock scandals to overbuilding to an economic recession that Richard Nixon blamed for his loss to John F. Kennedy. By the end of what Brunswick dubbed the "Golden Sixties," half of America's bowling centers were unprofitable. Bowling fell off a cliff in 1962 after a recession, stock speculation, antitrust legislation, new taxes, high equipment costs, overbuilding, and graft.

In 1959, the American Bowling Congress issued guidelines suggesting that the optimum number of bowling lanes was one lane for every five thousand people in the East, and one

The promotional album for Brunswick's sales conference, *The Golden Sixties*, was a record of the industrial musical the company staged to motivate their sales force to push the Gold Crown Line.

thousand people in California. As operators kept pushing beyond those numbers, observers suggested the industry was overbuilt, but new centers continued to open regularly.

During the peak of the bowling boom, there was a dizzying expansion in already saturated markets. In 1960, the country's twenty-two million bowlers spent $250 million annually on their sport—ten times as much as they spent attending every major league game the previous year. New all-night centers could open in an area full of competitors and still sell out the lanes, inspiring owners to keep expanding. The BPAA itself doubled in size between 1955 and 1960; similarly, the

number of alleys doubled between 1956 and 1959. In 1960, five hundred new alleys were in the planning stages in the San Francisco Bay area alone.

It seemed there were no limits. In 1959, Brunswick reported to shareholders, "There is no dearth of opportunities, for we have only to look out upon a world of expanding population and rising living standards—where people are determined to have more leisure time and to enjoy better education, better health, and wholesome recreation in a world at peace."

Boosters kept stoking the fires with predictions of unlimited growth. At the company's 1960 sales convention, singers urged salesmen to push the company's new line of equipment with lyrics promising that "The Gold Crown Line will be a halo around your head and a noose for the competition." They were a little out of control on that one.

Brunswick president B.E. Bensinger, who hunted with Ernest Hemingway and ran with the bulls, purchased an entire herd of racehorses in 1961 when company stock had shot up to $75 a share. He named them Gutter Ball, Strikes and Spares, Duck Pin, Candle Pin, Pin Setter, and Queen Pin. He was about to retire from the company his in-laws had founded in 1849, and all was good in the world.

And then it wasn't. In 1962, Brunswick's net profit dropped 53% and their stock collapsed in what was dubbed the "flash crash," the biggest market drop since the one that caused the Great Depression. "Corporate profits are not any better than they were five years ago," investor Warren Buffet said of the crash. "But stock prices are 50% higher." Brunswick profit had fallen from a high of $6.40 per share in 1958 to one cent in 1965.

A few months later, the business was over. Lacking new clients, Powers, Daly & DeRosa moved on to country clubs, motels, and shopping centers. Their bowling centers were sold, repossessed, and mistreated. "It's not at all uncommon for us to go back and find that they've ruined one of our buildings by plastering signs all over it," Daly said angrily. "One SOB, in particular, put up so many signs, the place looked like a banana split."

Suppliers, proprietors, and bowling associations were all trying desperately to save the industry. A former president of the BPAA warned, "No section of the country is immune from the specter of bankruptcy, price cutting, league stealing, and other desperate measures."

Drastic price cuts were unsuccessful. Craig Schene, whose family operated centers in California's Inland Empire, says, "just like they used to have gas wars, they'd lower the price just to get customers in there." He remembers, "Ten cents a line [when] an automatic [pinsetter] was about $10,000."

When customers couldn't make their monthly payments, manufacturers including Brunswick and AMF repossessed the bowling equipment and sometimes ended up

BOWLING IS BOOMING NOW

This headline from a recent issue of the Los Angeles Times tells *part* of the story. Bowling is America's most popular participation sport—by far.

1 person in every 8 in the United States bowls regularly (at least once a week). 20,000,000 regular bowlers in all!

it's just as popular in SOUTHERN CALIFORNIA!

There are about 220,000 regular league bowlers in Southern California, and an estimated 300,000 regular non-league bowlers!

There are nearly SIX times the number of regular bowlers in this area as the total of all golfers and tennis players—*combined*.

There are more than 3,000 bowling leagues in this area. An average of 30,000 teams that play at least once a week.

bowling at 3 A.M.!

There are so many bowlers here that many houses stay open 24 hours a day, 7 days a week.

If not *one* new family known to Southern California within the next year, existing facilities would often be strained to handle present bowlers.

The *need* for new bowling houses is great—and, as you'll see on the next page is growing GREATER BY THE DAY!

Regulators decried the promotional brochure for Wonder Bowl (1959, Daniel, Mann, Johnson and Mendenhall) as "flamboyant and misleading." The centers were funded by mom-and-pop investors reacting to television commercials for the project.

owning entire bowling centers as a result. By the end of the "Golden Sixties," 1,500 centers closed and half of America's bowling centers were unprofitable.

However, investors continued to be lured to the industry by the promise of quick riches. One ad promised that you could pay for a bowling center out of profits in approximately five years. In 1962, Beverly Hills developer

A mountain of Brunswick furniture crushed under the collapsing roof of the demolished Java Lanes (1958, Powers, Daly & DeRosa) in Long Beach, California in 2004.

Berman Swarttz opened a new center with financing from Lehman Brothers.

According to a government report, many owners and investors came to bowling through fandom. "They were inexperienced in running these operations and, in the case of absentee ownership, selected other bowling associates with similarly weak management to operate the alleys for them."

Some owners tried to save their businesses in ways that prompted government investigations. One proprietor in Northern California was accused of poaching leagues by offering free food, and operators soon upped the ante with cars and boats and $10,000 cash prizes paid for by insurance. When a flood of 300 games hit, the insurance companies canceled

the policies and refused to write any more. The State of California filed a lawsuit claiming there was a price fixing conspiracy.

Many new companies were formed with the intention of soliciting investors for building and operating bowling alleys. In 1963, the Securities and Exchange Commission (SEC) started investigating claims of financial PR firms disseminating false information about investing in bowling centers, spreading far rosier numbers than actually existed. The SEC investigated the annual reports of thirty bowling companies with publicly traded stock. In 1959, ten of the companies reported profits and three showed losses, but by 1963, six reported net profits and thirteen reported net losses. One investment group

Celebrity Sports Center (1960, Powers, Daly & DeRosa) was demolished in 1995. After Disney sold the property in 1979, it was renamed "Celebrity Fun Center." Wood from the bowling lanes was salvaged for a ballroom floor and one of the sign's big stars now sits atop Denver's Lumber Baron Inn.

offered one free share to anyone who could sell four shares for cash. Like so many others, when the Antelope Valley Recreation Center Company filed bankruptcy in 1967, all 800,000 shares of the stock were reported to be worthless. And then there was James Fallon and Wonder Bowl.

The Wall Street Journal crowned Fallon a financial kingpin in their 1961 publication *The New Millionaires* and *How They Made Their Fortunes*. His colorful advertising, contagious enthusiasm, and movie star good looks helped sell millions of shares in his Wonder Bowl before it crashed and burned in a spectacular bankruptcy.

According to his son, Bill Fallon, his father was "larger than life, a big personality, and a very handsome guy." Fallon was always confident if not always consistent. Bill remembers him as "a self-promoter ... but I don't think he was good at managing [his businesses] once they got off the ground."

Fallon joined the Navy the day after Pearl Harbor. When he left the navy for TWA, he thought he could work his way to the top in a couple of years but soon traded the airline for a newspaper job. His wife suggested he try working at an ad agency. Within two years he was vice president of the company and earning $150,000 a year.

He became board chairman and part owner of Filmaster, Inc, the television production

design of **WonderBowl** DOWNEY

a completely new architectural concept for bowling palaces

years-ahead DESIGN

- Unique "V" design with bank of alleys on *one* side of the "V" shape concourse and another bank of alleys on the other.
- This back-to-back design gives intimacy and "warmth" to the bowling area, reduces labor costs by about 40%. Makes a more efficient servicing and cleaning operation.
- Special built-in "TV" lanes for WonderBowl-Downey's extensive telecast activities. A "First" in this area.
- Custom-made portable tournament *bleacher facilities* for spectators.
- 3 permanent built-in camera booths for filming and TV activities.

years-ahead CUSTOMER SERVICE

- A la carte food service by uniformed attendants direct to bowler's benches.
- 24 hour coffee shop.
- The WonderBowl News, a newspaper.
- A superb restaurant and banquet facility.
- 7-table billiard room.
- Bowling sports shop.
- Children's playroom under supervision of registered attendant.
- Ball drilling service.

years-ahead CUSTOMER CONVENIENCES

- Subterranean ball returns. Avoids noise and hubbub.
- 3-channel sound system. For music and paging to one, a group, or all of 15 different areas.
- Continual FM music.
- Complete air-conditioning and humidified atmosphere.
- Custom-created pile carpeting throughout.
- TV tournaments.
- Weekly Bowling prizes.

Promotional brochure meant to sell stock in the second Wonder Bowl (1959, Daniel, Mann, Johnson and Mendenhall) in Downey.

company that produced hit shows including *Gunsmoke* and *Have Gun Will Travel*, and then he discovered bowling. He founded a construction company to build his projects and a real estate concern to buy the land. He started additional companies that would handle maintenance, purchasing, and operations for his projects.

He even launched a securities company to sell stock in his own corporation and a subsidiary that would train salesmen. For his efforts, he kept one share for each one sold by the company. One article described him as "a promoter whose business, basically, is organizing speculative ventures."

Architect Lee Linton (who would later go to jail for financial crimes at a mob-ridden Vegas casino) teamed up with Fallon to build the Millionaires Club in West Hollywood, a swanky private night spot in baroque googie style. The club featured rococo decor, with ornate chandeliers and marble nymphs. In order to finance such a lavish endeavor, he started selling advance memberships to potential members. Hugh Hefner's Playboy Club, another private institution down the Sunset Strip, sued Fallon, forcing him to return funds to investors, even though he had already spent the money on construction.

Fallon had already built a luxurious motor hotel with restaurant and lounge near Vandenberg Air Force Base in Santa Maria, and Wonder Fair, a proto WalMart, near Covina Bowl, and knew the suburban markets were ripe for more bowling. "Everything points to our country's going on the greatest recreational holiday in history," he said in 1959 before announcing what was to be a chain of posh bowling palaces.

The TV ads for Wonder Bowl were aimed at what we now call retail investors or nonprofessionals, who bought stock with their own money. "I spent $5,000 a week on television advertising for Wonder Bowl and completely revolutionized the stock sales business overnight," Fallon explained.

There was no direct pitch in the TV ad, just a number to call for more information. He captured the names of callers and sent out an enthusiastic brochure, then a call, and hopefully an in-home visit. "A good 70% of folks never owned stock before," Fallon said. "We make it really easy for people to buy." Wonder Bowl Anaheim opened in 1958 and a massive sixty-four-lane house opened a year later in Downey. Fallon was the president of both companies and owned 30% of the stock. Seven thousand individuals invested in the two centers and they were enormous and magnificent.

Fallon's fantasies came to life over and over and he allowed mere mortals to walk through his opulent worlds filled with wonders. The kind of wonders that get people indicted. By 1961, they had sold almost two million shares and touted future locations in Compton, Covina, and Norwalk. In a scheme reminiscent of the Millionaire's Club, Fallon came up with a "Country Club Plan" where members would pay monthly dues for unlimited free play as well as "exclusive social functions."

Fallon and his financial partners were hit with multiple felony fraud charges, including using unqualified salesmen without suitable training and "intensive telephone, radio, television, and direct mail solicitation, including the distribution of flamboyant and misleading brochures, advertisements and other sales literature," he was also charged with switching securities within the accounts of investors. The SEC investigated Fallon and revoked his stock broker's license because he violated federal laws when he sold speculative stock even though he was insolvent.

Stockholders claimed fraud after the companies failed to issue financial reports in 1965 and 1966. The state Attorney General was investigating stockholders' allegations that funds from Wonder Bowl were siphoned

into other holdings. The company soon filed petitions in US district court asking for temporary relief from creditors while planning a reorganization to avert bankruptcy.

The Wonder Bowls were also investigated by the IRS for not paying their income taxes. The IRS seized the properties and litigation dragged on into the mid-1970s when the organization's charter was suspended and its assets liquidated.

A more scandalous story surrounded the creation and subsequent forced bankruptcy of the lavish La Mesa Bowl in San Diego.

AMF, which owned a second trust deed and mortgage on the equipment, forced a bankruptcy sale in October 1965, but these owners were different. Frank M. "Big Frank" Matranga and Joseph Matranga broke ground two years earlier with over a million dollars borrowed from Jimmy Hoffa's Teamsters Union Pension Fund.

When the La Mesa City Council learned of the connection between the Matrangas and Detroit mafioso John "Papa John" Priziola, they denied their request for a liquor license based on "unsavory backgrounds." Their

Abandoned to nature, the Orange Bowl (1957, Underhill & Wagner) in Rialto, California, awaits its fate. ◆ Opposite: Wonder Bowl (1959, Daniel, Mann, Johnson and Mendenhall) was a fantastical confection of geometry and color in suburban Anaheim, California.

associate Vincent Provenzano was president of the newly formed La Mesa Bowl Corporation and was able to obtain the liquor license before quickly transferring most of the stock and the license back to the Matrangas.

The Alcoholic Beverage Control Department (ABCD) soon revoked the license and the brothers needed it back. In March of 1965, Dominic Tavaglione, a long-time friend of the Matrangas and real estate broker who had been trying to sell the property, arranged to take two of the three members of the ABCD Appeals Board to dinner at the bowling alley's lavish restaurant.

Cousin Frank A. Matranga, who had been convicted of land fraud in San Bernardino County, arrived with what the *Valley Times* called "party girls." The same paper reported that the Matrangas paid the tab for the evening out and hotel rooms, which was covertly documented by law enforcement. California Governor Pat Brown ordered an investigation.

"Whoever gave this kind of information about them should be shot," said Joe Matranga. "This is a public place. What's the matter with them coming here? I didn't even know

Frank Matranga, at his grand jury indictment. Frank and Joe Matranga transferred their interest in La Mesa Bowl (1963, architect unknown) to a dummy corporation.

who they were until yesterday." Despite further appeals, La Mesa Bowl was not granted a new liquor license and the Teamsters started foreclosure proceedings on a mortgage with an unpaid balance higher than the original loan.

The bowling industry was in a financial freefall through the 1960s. Bowlers also faced continued racial discrimination after the passage of the Civil Rights Act of 1964.

When customers left, the centers tried to adapt, employing myriad techniques to expand their audience. In 1963, Pasadena Bowling Center started a new "Moonlight Bowl" on Sunday. "We turn all the house lights off except for different colored lights over the pins," said manager Jim La Grutta. "There are black and red colored pins in each group that are worth cash if they fall in a strike. And there's also a gold pin . . . if it doesn't fall one night, the amount goes up the next time." Not to be outdone, in 1966 the Poway Bowl set up a carnival in their parking lot which featured helicopter rides and a battle of the bands.

The clientele was changing. Bob Jacobs, who played with the Vi-Counts at the

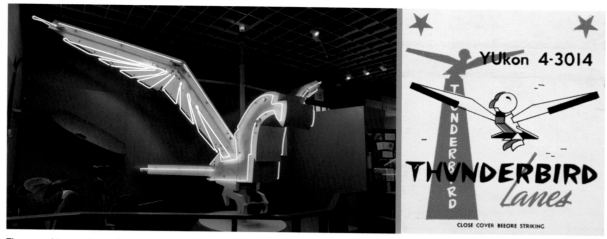

The neon shines again on the enormous mythical creature that once overlooked Thunderbird Lanes (1959, William Wong) in Ontario, California. The sculpture has been restored and is a highlight of the Ontario Museum of History & Art.

World War II generation differed from their children. Those were folks likely to stay at the same job for a lifetime, own homes in the new suburbs, and become invested in their new communities filled with other young families like themselves. Of the Boomer and Gen Xers that followed, Putnam writes: "It is as though the post-war generations were exposed to some anti-civic X-ray that permanently and increasingly rendered them less likely to connect with the community." Then the digital divide hit. Even children playing video games together could be alone in their separate rooms miles or countries away. Losing all of these connections affects more than just bowling. According to Putnam, social ties "foster sturdy norms of reciprocity. I'll do this for you now, in the expectation that you (or perhaps someone else) will return the favor." Putnam's book seems extra relevant in increasingly divided times.

Large recreation centers took up huge swaths of increasingly valuable land that developers couldn't wait to get their hands on. Even though Northridge Bowl was doing a good business, "the owner of the property made us an offer we couldn't refuse," said owner Robert Feuchter, who had just signed a twenty year lease. "He found he had a better use for the land." These prime sites along highways with vast oceans of parking could accommodate a big box shopping center or a swath of high-density apartments. Some early investors that owned their land retired as millionaires. Actor Joe Kirkwood, Jr., who starred in several *Joe Palooka* movies, opened his Studio City center in 1958 with a $5,000 investment, and sold it two years later for $3.8 million. "This is not a tribute to my business head," he laughed. "But to the fabulous rise in California real estate."

Since most alleys were built during the

boom between 1957 and 1962, their thirty-year leases started coming up for renewal in the late 1980s, and those on fifty-year leases became vulnerable in the early 2000s. "Land values have gone up so high," Nate Rosenfeld, an owner of Canoga Park Bowl said, "that, at lease renewal time, landlords want to get a lot more rent or turn it into another business." One owner noted that he could earn more from selling his lease than he could in ten years of operation.

"From 1963 to 1968, centers were closing because they were overbuilt," said proprietor Mark Spiegel, whose Active West alleys were

A later-in-life view of the dynamic steel entrance canopy at Anaheim Bowl (1959, Powers, Daly & DeRosa). The icon was kept in excellent condition until the center closed in 1988.

once Southern California's largest chain. "But, from 1973 to '83, the majority of centers closed because they had lost their leases." By that time, four or five centers were closing every year in California. Closures were rarely announced more than a few weeks in advance. Even if the end was rumored for years, longtime staff, league members, and neighbors were often surprised that their institution was headed for the chopping block.

The closure of a beloved center is a loss to the community that forms around it. If owners were strictly pragmatic, others tried to do what was best for the neighborhood, or the fans, or the game itself. "Statistics show that when bowling centers close, approximately twenty to twenty-five percent of the people who attend regularly quit bowling," lamented Nave Lanes's manager Paul Panholzer. "We've contacted each and every person who bowls here and tried to get them involved in another place."

A family squabble doomed Willow Grove Park Lanes. The massive facility was converted to retail space themed to reflect the early twentieth century amusement park the bowling alley had replaced. "Today, the great turquoise, concrete beak of Willow Grove lanes upstages the red brick nostalgia of the new Willow Grove Park," critic Thomas Hine wrote after the center closed in 1983. "The mall seeks to evoke memories of a past that never was which makes it a characteristic building of our time. It's neighbor, the bowling alley, is an extravagant work of an era that many people still remember, a time that looked to the future rather than to the past."

Some centers were repurposed into new uses. The massive Bronco Bowl in Dallas was reconfigured as a concert venue, hosting major acts like David Bowie, Bruce Springsteen, and U2. But even that reuse couldn't survive the big box era, and it was replaced by a Home Depot. After a years-long preservation battle, San Diego's Bowlero was demolished by Home Depot. Even Celebrity Sports Center near Denver eventually fell for a Staples, a Whole Foods, and . . . a Home Depot.

Closures due to COVID-19 doomed many other centers around the country. Bowling, like many businesses, was hard hit during the shutdown. When Georgia allowed bowling alleys to reopen sooner than the rest of the country, it was easy comedy for late talk show hosts like *The Daily Show*'s Trevor Noah, who said it was like asking "people to join a competitive sneezing league." Cloverleaf Bowl in Fremont, which opened in 1959, was one of many to never reopen after the pandemic. Patrons cried when the doors of Poway Fun Bowl were locked and it was set to be replaced by two hundred luxury apartments. Southport Lanes in Chicago permanently closed in 2021 after operating for nearly a century. Bowlers,

The enormous porte cochere at Willow Grove Park Lanes (1961, Powers, Daly & DeRosa) near Philadelphia, was chopped off and the space transformed for retail use after the center closed in 1983.

Sepulveda Bowl (1957, Martin Stern Jr.) closed and reopened as a large appliance store in 1969, then was resurrected as Mission Hills Bowl in 1975. Closing for good in 2015, the building, with its distinctive angled web-lightener I-beams, was restored as a Ross Dress for Less.

community members, and preservationists sometimes win, but it's a mixed bag.

The Los Angeles Conservancy Modern Committee and the Coalition to Save Holiday Bowl spent years trying to rescue the historically, culturally, and architecturally significant Holiday Bowl. The *New York Times* wrote that the center "brought together Nisei survivors of World War II internment camps, working-class Blacks from the offspring of Negro bowling leagues, and young white preservation activists." Former Holiday Bowl coffee shop waitress Jacqueline Sowell said, "It's like a United Nations in there. Our employees are Hispanic, white, Black, Japanese, Thai, Filipino. I've served grits to as many Japanese customers as I do Black. We've learned from each other and

given to each other." The Los Angeles Historic-Cultural Monument was largely demolished, but is memorialized through public art and a restored coffee shop.

Bowlium, Bel Mateo Bowl, and Country Club Lanes in California and 300 Bowl in Phoenix remain as the sole operating examples of the magnificent mid-century centers designed by masters Powers, Daly & DeRosa. Although Covina Bowl closed in 2017, it was listed on the California Register of Historical Resources and eligible for the National Register of Historic Places. Much of the building was demolished for new condominiums, but a compromise was reached where the major character-defining features, from the towering neon sign to the zigzag porte cochere, monumental pyramid entrance, and coffee

A coalition of community groups rallied to save the Holiday Bowl (1958, Armet & Davis) after it closed in 2000.

shop were restored under the exacting supervision of historian Jennifer Mermilliod who numbered each piece of flagstone and revealed long-forgotten design elements. The landmark was unveiled with an exuberant party featuring Edsels and roller-skating carhops. The exterior and sign for Friendly Hills Lanes look much as they did in 1956, but the lanes are occupied by an Aldi supermarket. The neon letters "BOWL" were swapped out with "SHOP."

The rose-colored concrete parabolic domes of the 1962 Rose Bowl in Tulsa were restored as a sports and community center for underserved youth in 2012. Basketball, football, and soccer are played inside the cavernous structure, but as at Covina Bowl, a noncompete clause in the sale agreement forbids bowling.

The out-of-this-world conversion of Silva Lanes in Santa Fe, New Mexico, into the wildly successful "artmusement" park Meow Wolf has made headlines all over the world. *Game of Thrones* author George R. R. Martin collaborated with the art collective on a multimillion-dollar renovation that turned the

Top: Covina Bowl (1956, Powers, Daly & DeRosa) kicked off bowling's mid-century renaissance. After the landmark closed in 2017, Trumark Homes restored the building's character-defining features as part of a townhouse development. ◆ Below: Friends of the Covina Bowl celebrated its sixtieth anniversary with a birthday party hosted by Cary Stratton, whose newscaster father Gil Stratton did the honors in 1956.

lanes into a wonderland of glowing caves, an enchanted forest, a life-size mastodon skeleton with musical ribs, and space age corridors crafted by more than one hundred artists. The former bowling alley is large enough to hold classrooms, artists' studios, galleries, event spaces, and room for other nonprofits. The group has since expanded to locations in Las Vegas, Denver, and Dallas.

Mira Mesa Lanes won an eleventh-hour reprieve when professional bowler Missy Parkin announced on Facebook Live that she

and her partners bought the facility in 2021. "It's been my dream since I was a little girl to own a bowling center," she announced. "We didn't want bowling to die in San Diego, so we are so happy we could help save it." Longtime Mira Mesa bowler Angel PinaHardin said, "It's not only the sport, but it's the camaraderie you feel when you get together with your bowling family. It's the tradition of passing bowling on to my kids."

America's pop culture love affair with bowling never waned, even as the number of bowling centers continued to decline. Every sitcom character since the 1950s seems to visit the lanes, from Fred Flintstone and Ralph Kramden to that talking horse Mr. Ed. More contemporary films have portrayed a game of bowling as the ideal of a bygone era. In the 1998 film *Pleasantville*, the opening scene depicts idealized 1950s bowlers in three different lanes, all picking up a spare from a 7-10 split. The central idea of the 2000s TV comedy *Ed* is that a New York lawyer can go back to his hometown bowling alley after misadventures in the big city. Perhaps the most famous bowling film of all was 1998's *The Big Lebowski*.

The lights are on, but nobody's home at Southwest Bowl (1958, architect unknown), seen shortly after it closed in 2008. The G4 show *Human Wrecking Balls* graphically destroyed much of the building. The remains were restored by a non-profit community group.

In recent years, a new crop of bowling alleys have breathed life back into the industry. "From the mid-'60s through the '70s there was a major fall," says Spiegel of Active West. "But when computerized scoring came in there was a boom. It brought other things like bumpers and an emphasis on birthday parties." After Brunswick introduced black lights, lasers, fog machines, and fluorescent balls in the '90s, some 80% of American bowling centers offered some form of musically enhanced "glow bowling" for their young adult patrons. Instead of a funky and affordable pastime for the whole family, many alleys have gone upscale and positioned themselves as a date night destination. One reporter described the transition as "draft beer has been replaced with the martini. Hot dogs are out and sushi is in. The democratic, all-inclusive, mid-century bowling center has been replaced with the ultra-hip, uberglam."

Splitsville opened their first location in 2003 with the slogan "reinventing America's game." Their luxury lanes in Anaheim feature six hundred dining seats, two craft cocktail bars, and a stage for live music. Palace Bowling Lanes in Houston, Texas, sat vacant for two years before being revamped into Palace Social. The forty-lane center was transformed into a family amusement park with fine dining, bars, arcade games, a dark ride theater, multi-sport simulator bays, and virtual reality gaming. The center also preserved eight bowling lanes on a raised platform in the back of the main room.

300 Bowl (1958, Powers, Daly & DeRosa), a.k.a. Bowlero Christown in Phoenix, Arizona maintains much of its original integrity on the outside and operates as a modern Bowlero inside.

BOWLARAMA

Visitors examine artifacts from bowling's golden age at *Bowlarama*, an exhibition at the A+D Architecture and Design museum in 2014.

The industry was taking another pivot, and one up-and-comer in particular was poised to transform the world of bowling. Bowlero, the company Tom Shannon started in 1992 by reimagining the rundown Bowlmor Lanes in New York as an upscale socializing spot, has grown into the world's largest bowling operator, with over 12,000 lanes. The company purchased AMF and Brunswick Corporation's bowling center business, uniting the two competitors for the first time. In 2019, they acquired the Professional Bowlers Association (PBA), and, in 2023, luxury competitor Lucky Strike. Mr. Shannon says he loves vintage bowling centers and wants to keep the survivors thriving in this age of luxury bowling. "If there's only going to be one steward of these old bowling alleys, I'm glad it's going to be me," he told this writer on the lanes. "I love these places as much as you do."

Salt Lake City designer Grady Huff, who redesigned Mar Vista Lanes in West Angeles for Bowlero, describes his inspiration as a "road trip to Baja," but the concept looks back on the entire twentieth century as a toy box from which to select design motifs, from *Dogtown and Z-Boys* surf to Lava Lamps to Ms. Pac-Man. It's all mixed up and comes out feeling a little like bowling poolside at the Ace Hotel in Palm Springs. The young staff is wildly enthusiastic and seems genuinely excited to be there, and they're everywhere. You won't have to wait long to enjoy your order of Fon-Dude or Enchill-Outas.

What should people make of these transformations that brought the modern bowling alley into the twenty-first century? Nonagenarian Irv Noren went back to see what had become of his namesake alley in Pasadena as it became a Bowlero in 2019. "Man, I went by one day and they're tearing it up, and I said, 'I'm Irv Noren.' They knew my name. It was unbelievable. I walked in that sucker and I couldn't believe what a job they did. It didn't have the atmosphere of a bowling alley. It was beautiful but it felt like, I don't know, not a bowling alley. It looked more like a nightclub and by the time you go further, they got lights flashing and all that stuff."

Bowling has transformed and reinvented itself many times over the decades but still attracts kids in the summertime, seniors in the morning, and first dates on Friday nights. The new era of luxury bowling has been compared to a boozy Hollywood nightclub filled with bars and bowlers partying on the lanes. Oh wait, that's how *Life* magazine described them in 1958. The more things change.

Bowlero Corporation acquired competitor Lucky Strike in 2023. This location in Moorpark, California, opened in 2024 and showcases the high energy nightclub appeal that excites a new generation of young bowlers.

A GUIDE TO THE REMAINING MID-CENTURY BOWLING CENTERS

Grab your bowling bag and head out on an expedition to our selected list of America's best remaining mid-century bowling centers. While we didn't include early twentieth century icons like Holler House in in Milwaukee, or glamorous retro makeovers like Avondale Bowl in Chicago, we heartily encourage you to seek them all out and roll a game. We'll see you on the lanes!

ARKANSAS
Holiday Entertainment, Texarkana

ARIZONA
Bowlero Christown, Phoenix
Let it Roll, Phoenix

CALIFORNIA
Bel Mateo Bowl, San Mateo
Boulevard Lanes, Petaluma
Bowlium, Montclair
Burney Bowl, Burney
Corbin Bowl, Tarzana
Country Club Bowl, San Rafael
Country Club Lanes, Sacramento
Danville Bowl, Danvile
Del Rio Lanes, Downey
Bowlero El Dorado, Westchester
Bowlero, Goleta
Freeway Lanes, Selma
4th Street Bowl, San Jose
Gage Bowl, Huntington Park
Shatto 39 Lanes, Los Angeles
La Habra "300" Bowl, La Habra
Linbrook Bowl, Anaheim
Monterey Lanes, Monterey
Pacific Ave. Bowl, Stockton
Parkway Bowl, El Cajon
Rancho Bowl, Santa Maria
Simi Bowl, Simi Valley
Surf Bowl, Oceanside
Valley Center Bowl, Salinas
West Lane Bowl, Stockton
Yosemite Lanes, Modesto

COLORADO
Crown Lanes, Denver

FLORIDA
Orange Bowl Lanes, Kissimmee
Ten Pin Lanes, South Pasadena

IDAHO
Caldwell Bowl, Caldwell
Owyhee Lanes, Homedale
Pop'n Pins, Preston

ILLINOIS
Arrowhead Lanes, Champaign
Bel-Air Bowl, Belleville
Castaways Bowl, Calumet City
Diversey River Bowl, Chicago
Metro Bowl, Crystal Lake
Town Hall Bowl, Cicero

INDIANA
Cressmoor Lanes, Hobart
Norwood Bowl, Alexandria
Plaza Lanes, Connersville
Wawasee Lanes, Syracuse

IOWA
Arrowhead Bowl, Keokuk

KANSAS
Gage Bowl, Topeka
Holiday Bowl, Augusta
Starlite Lanes, McPherson

KENTUCKY
Bowlarama, Danville
Southland Lanes, Lexington
Ten Pin Strike & Spare, Louisville

LOUISIANA
Holiday Lanes, Bossier City

MAINE
Big 20, Scarborough

MARYLAND
Rinaldi Lanes, Riverdale

MICHIGAN
Bowlero Lanes, Royal Oak
Clique Lanes, Grand Rapids
Crestwood Bowl, St. Louis
Garden Bowl, Detroit
Bowl-E-Drome, Howell
Sherman Bowling Center, Muskegon
Town 'n Country Lanes, Westland

MINNESOTA
Memory Lanes, Minneapolis

MISSOURI
Crestwood Bowl, St. Louis
GraceStar Lanes, Carthage
New Blue Springs Bowl, Blue Springs
Sterling Lanes, Sugar Creek
Tropicana Lanes, Richmond Heights

MONTANA
Little's Lanes, Great Falls
Sunset Lanes, Billings

NEBRASKA
Chops Bowling, Omaha

NEVADA
Boulder City Bowl, Boulder City

NEW JERSEY
Bowler City, Hackensack
Hanover Lanes, East Hanover
Parkway Lanes, Elmwood Park
Pinsetter Bowl, Merchantville
Playdrome, Toms River

NEW MEXICO
Bel Air Bowl, Hobbs
Gal-A-Bowl, Gallup

NEW YORK
Boulevard Bowl, Schenectady
Flamingo Bowl, Liverpool
Gun Post Lanes, Bronx

NORTH CAROLINA
Sky Lanes, Asheville

NORTH DAKOTA
Red Ray Lanes, Grand Forks
Ten Spot Bowling, Mandan

OHIO
Capri Lanes, Dayton
Echo Lanes, Warren
Yorktown Lanes, Cleveland

OREGON
Caveman Bowl, Grants Pass
Northgate Bowl, Salem

PENNSYLVANIA
Dutch Lanes, Ephrata

SOUTH DAKOTA
Eastway Bowl, Sioux Falls
Fair City Lanes, Huron
Sport Bowl, Sioux Falls
Suburban Lanes, Sioux Falls
Village Bowl, Aberdeen

TENNESSEE
Holiday Lanes, Johnson City

TEXAS
Corsicana Park Lanes, Corsicana
Paris Lanes, Paris
Stadium Lanes, San Angelo

UTAH
Bonwood Bowling Center, South Salt Lake
Cedar Bowling Center, Cedar City
Dixie Bowl, St. George
Holiday Lanes, Heber City

WASHINGTON
Kent Bowl, Kent
Tiger Bowl, Battle Ground
Westside Lanes, Olympia

WISCONSIN
Oregon Bowl, Oregon
Rand's Lanes, Rice Lake

WYOMING
El Mark-O Lanes, Casper
Silver Spur Lanes, Lander

ABOUT THE AUTHORS

CHRIS NICHOLS is a longtime preservationist and senior editor at *Los Angeles* magazine. For many years he worked with the Los Angeles Conservancy Modern Committee, serving a term as chairman of the group. In addition to creating tours, exhibitions, and lectures about historic Los Angeles, Nichols has advocated for endangered buildings all over Southern California including the Cinerama Dome and the world's oldest McDonald's in Downey. His books include *Walt Disney's Disneyland* for Taschen and *The Leisure Architecture of Wayne McAllister*. He writes the Ask Chris column in *Los Angeles* magazine and has served on the board of Hollywood Heritage.

An award-winning historian and advocate, **ADRIENE BIONDO** grew up in the lost world of twenty-four hour bowling alleys and coffee shops. As a former chair of the Los Angeles Conservancy's Modern Committee and past president of the Museum of Neon Art, there's never a moment when she isn't working to preserve the magic of mid-century buildings and neon signs. She has initiated nominations for many key landmarks including the Capitol Records building in Hollywood, and Johnie's Broiler in Downey. Adriene has written four books with John Eng, and is a feature writer and photographer for *CA-Modern* architecture magazine.

Bowlarama: The Architecture of Mid-Century Bowling

By Chris Nichols with Adriene Biondo

Copyright © 2024 Chris Nichols

Design by Amy Inouye, Future Studio

10 9 8 7 6 5 4 3 2 1

ISBN-13 978-1-62640-131-0

Library of Congress Cataloging-in-Publication Data is available

Published by Angel City Press at Los Angeles Public Library
www.angelcitypress.com

Printed in Canada

Norwalk Bowl (1955, David T. Witherly) featured twenty-four lanes running twenty-four hours a day alongside the Safari Room lounge.

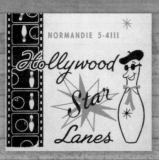

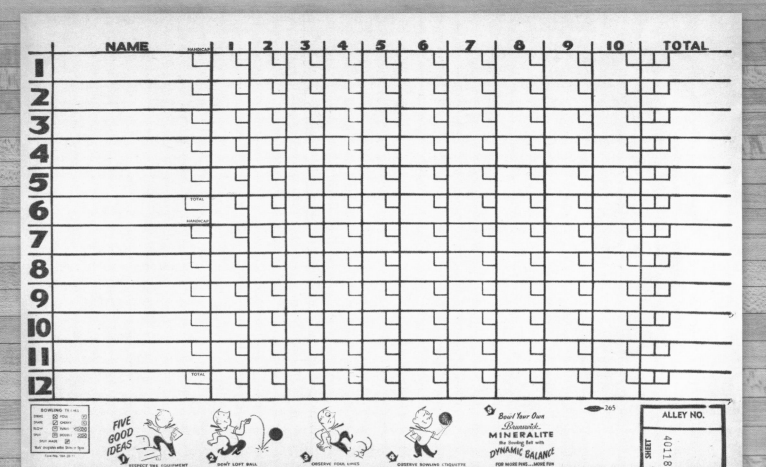

ALMA BOWL 32 LANES
355 W. ALMA ST. SAN JOSE, CALIF.
Close Cover Before Striking

ACORN BOWL

never closes
ANAHEIM BOWL

the Family that Plays together stays together
ARROWHEAD Lanes
SAN BERNARDINO
Close Cover Before Striking

32 AUTOMATIC LANES
Beautiful ANN DARLING BOWL
1661 McKee Road San Jose, Calif.
CL 8-0950
CLOSE COVER FOR SAFETY

Victor 9-4601
Banning BOWL
COFFEE SHOP
COCKTAILS
CHILDREN'S PLAYROOM
1309 WEST RAMSEY STREET
BANNING • CALIFORNIA

LEARN TO BOWL
Inquire About Our Free Instruction & Bowling Program For Beginners!
Phone: TUrner 9-0355

FRONTIER 6-6992
40 LANES
BEACH BOWL
HERMOSA BEACH
CLOSE COVER BEFORE STRIKING

House with the Continental Flair
BelAir LANES

DINING and DANCING in the 300 Club
PLAYROOM COFFEE SHOP PRO SHOP
Bel Aire BOWL COCKTAILS
3900 BEL AIRE PLAZA NAPA, CALIFORNIA
MONARCH MATCH COMPANY, SAN JOSE, CALIFORNIA

MODERN BOWLING AND DINING FACILITIES.....
SAMOA LANES
5th & BROADWAY SANTA MONICA, CALIF.
EXbrook 3-0293
Close Cover Before Striking

Bowl and Dine
at WILLOW GROVE PARK LANES
"The Bowling Palace of the World"
Please Close Cover Before Striking

FIreside 1-2616
Bel Mateo BOWL
43rd & OLYMPIC AVENUES SAN MATEO
Close Cover Before Striking

Bowling Square
CLOSE COVER BEFORE STRIKING

Bowlero bowling
A NEW WORLD OF ENTERTAINMENT

LIBERTY 5-2662
The Beautiful Rose BOWL
765 SEBASTOPOL ROAD SANTA ROSA, CALIFORNIA
Close Cover Before Striking

Automatic Pinspotters
LANES BOWLING COCKTAILS
Pomona BOWLING CENTER
LYcoming 2-0672
300 SO. SAN ANTONIO • POMONA, CALIF.

Gardena Bowl
MEnlo 4-1244
15707 SOUTH VERMONT GARDENA, CALIFORNIA

Bowlium
"BOWL FOR FUN"
4666 HOLT BLVD. MONTCLAIR, CALIF.

YOrkshire 8-0085
GOLOBIC'S Camino BOWL
2025 EL CAMINO REAL • MOUNTAIN VIEW
Close Cover Before Striking

GOLDEN ST LAN
425 GOLDEN STAT (At Intersection H and 24 St.)
BAKERSFIEL CALIFORNIA

BOWLING • COFFEE • COCKTAIL
BILLIARDS • SHOP • LOUNGE
Hollywood Recreation
1539 N.VINE ST.
HO. 6331
CLOSE COVER BEFORE STRIKING

WHITEHALL 8-2651
SANDS BOWL
43233 SIERRA HIGHWAY LANCASTER, CALIFORNIA
CLOSE COVER BEFORE STRIKING

CRestwood 9-2388
300 Bowl
FOR PERFECT BOWLING
BETHANY HOME ROAD AT 19th AVE. PHOENIX, ARIZ.
Close Cover Before Striking

DR 6-4495
RHEEM BOWL
489 MORAGA RD. RHEEM, CALIF.
Close Cover Before Striking

DAvis 3-9333
FAculty 1-4091
Missile Bowl
1280 REDONDO BEACH BLVD. GARDENA, CALIFORNIA
CLOSE COVER BEFORE STRIKING

VAndike
COFFEE SHOP FOUNT
30 ALLEYS
NINTH and GR